# Designing and Making Rocking Horses

# Designing and Making
# Rocking Horses

Margaret Spencer

THE CROWOOD PRESS

First published in 2001 by
The Crowood Press Ltd
Ramsbury, Marlborough
Wiltshire SN8 2HR

Paperback edition 2009

**British Library Cataloguing-in-Publication Data**
A catalogue record for this book is available from the British Library.

ISBN 978 1 84797 108 1

**Acknowledgements**
With thanks to Sarah Drew, Victoria Shearing, Nigel Vincent, daughter Marion and husband Ron.

Typeset by Annette Findlay
Printed and bound in Singapore by Craft Print International Ltd

# CONTENTS

# A Note on Conversions and Safety

There are strict rules to follow when making rocking horses, with regard to child safety. The horses must be well constructed, with no sharp points or exposed screws or nails; the same applies to all accessories. If horse hair is used for the mane or tail, it must have come from a healthy horse, and be properly cleaned and cured. All leather must be vegetable tanned and paints must be child-safe.

At the time of writing, two forms of measurement are in use. Officially, metric measurements – millimetres and centimetres – are used, however many people prefer the old imperial measurements. To help the latter, below is a conversion guide.

To convert centimetres to inches, divide by 2.54 for an exact conversion. For example:

| | | |
|---|---|---|
| 0.32cm (3.2mm) | = | ⅛in |
| 0.64cm (6.4mm) | = | ¼in |
| 0.92cm (9.2mm) | = | ⅜in |
| 1.27cm (12.7mm) | = | ½in |
| 1.59cm (15.9mm) | = | ⅝in |
| 1.9cm (19mm) | = | ¾in |
| 2.54cm (25.4mm) | = | 1in |

An approximate 'working' conversion is 25cm (250mm) = 12in.

The dimensions of pieces of wood are given as length × width × depth throughout the book.

The diagrams in this book are not to scale; only the actual plans are to scale.

# THE ROCKING HORSE IN THE TWENTIETH CENTURY

The start of the twentieth century saw a boom in rocking horses. Leading the field were G. & J. Lines, Ayres, Collinson & Sons, and many smaller firms, all of which made a significant contribution to the industry.

The motor car was still in its infancy and railways were only just being built, so the horse was the main mode of transport.

And while the rocking horse was regarded primarily as a toy, it also provided a good means of exercise during bad weather, and was used to help teach the children of nobility and the new middle class to ride horses.

The rocking horses were made in non-automated factories, in which the workers stood at long benches. Each man had a

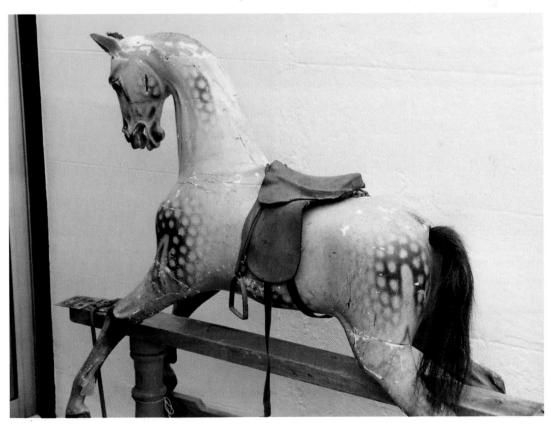

*Circa 1900 by Ayres. Considered the best horses ever made by many makers.*

*Collinson & Sons.*

different piece of the horse to make, and the horse was assembled at the end of the line. The First World War saw a great decline in their manufacture as men went off to war. Many small firms closed down, and of those that remained open, relying on an older workforce, many took on war work instead.

In the 1920s, there were many changes. Ladies were now allowed to ride astride a horse, so pommels on the saddles of both real and rocking horses disappeared. New designs were tried, mostly on stands, using leaf or coiled springs, some with complicated struts, but in time these rusted and became a hazard. New firms such as Leeway sprang up, but the quality of rocking horses deteriorated.

The three sons of G. Lines (whose company closed in 1931) broke away from the parent company to set up on their own as Lines Bros. Trading as Triang Toys, or Triangtois, they were one of the few companies to maintain the standard of their horses, although even Triang horses had shorter heads (which helped to identify them).

The boom years were definitely over. There were new 'toys' for both young and old. With the coming of good roads, there were more cars, motorbikes, bicycles, buses, trains and trams. For the children there were pedal cars and tricycles or bicycles. The horse was no longer king, merely a luxury, and stables were turned into garages. In addition, the 1920s saw the

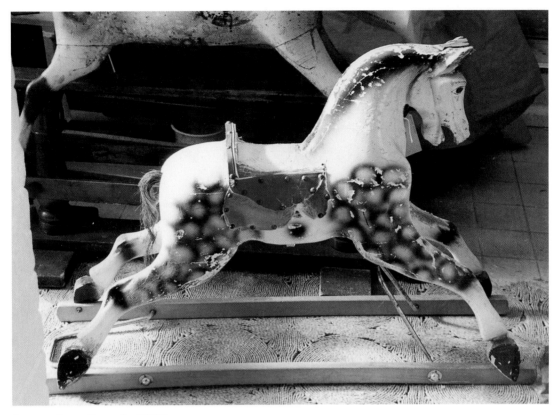

*Leeway horse from the 1920s.*

lean years of the Depression, and rocking horses have always been an expensive toy. Skin-covered and some fabric-covered horses were imported from Germany at this time.

Those manufacturers that did survive were the ones that diversified into prams and other toys; the small firms that specialized in rocking horses had all but disappeared by the time of the Second World War.

In the 1940s, the manufacture of rocking horses stopped except for one or two amateurs. The raw materials simply could not be found for luxury items, as factories such as Triang again went over to war work. Others such as F. H. Ayres were taken over.

After the war, interest in the horse as an animal for leisure built once more. Television helped enormously, as show jumping, pony trekking, horse racing, hunting, pony clubs, and so on, were often shown, and the public interest was aroused.

There was a corresponding rise in interest in rocking horses, and companies began to produce them again; one of the early post-war makers was James Bosworthwick, followed by Andrew Booth (my father) who inspired me to design my own in the early 1960s. Some firms had new ideas and tried new materials. Triang made small, tubular, metal-framed horses as well as their wooden ones until they ceased trading in 1972. Sebel, trading under the name Mobo, made a pressed

*Pre-1940 German stuffed horse with cow-hide cover.*

metal horse with springs, however these went out of fashion, and there is doubt as to whether they would have passed the tough safety regulations for toys that exist today.

The Trogen Horse Company made a synthetic fur-covered horse, an updated version of the fur fabric horse of the first half of the century. The latter consisted of a screwed wooden frame and head stuffed with straw or wood straw, covered with fur fabric, such as 'Teddy bear' fur, and mounted on a platform on rockers. Later the stuffing became foam. Between the 1950s and 1980s, Ragamuffin Toys and Pegasus & Crew Ltd both produced horses with the traditional screwed wooden frame, however, with vigorous rocking these soon came loose and fell apart. Merrythought, who were already well known

for their excellent stuffed toys, added stuffed horses to their catalogue in 1960 and changed the interior frame to metal, which was stronger. They could be produced in quantities, they were easy to manufacture, light to move, very cuddly, and the price was right – an absolute winner. This latest version could also be purchased on a swinger stand.

Few of these firms had more than a dozen people working for them, partly because new tools had taken some of the tedium out of making wooden rocking horses, and therefore fewer people were needed, but it was still very much 'hands on' work. Stevenson Bros, the owners of which were taught the craft by their uncle, James Bosworthwick, really caught the bug and became leading makers. As well as many other types of rocking horse, they

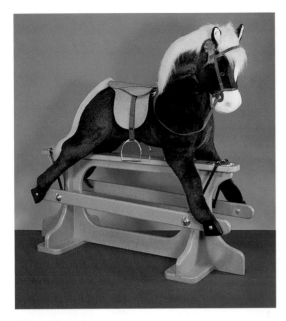

*Merrythoughts.*

made very good copies of Victorian horses, even adding woodworm (pseudo only) if required.

Anthony Dew in Yorkshire produced a horse at reasonable cost – with very striking dappling which was easily recognizable. He also made other items and launched a rocking horse magazine.

In the 1980s, another new material was used successfully. Tridas of Bath, and Relic, among others, made the whole horse exterior from fibreglass, which was attached to a wooden frame inside. The mouldings were often taken straight from old Victorian wooden horses, which made them look very impressive, and it was hard to detect the difference until one looked very closely. They were also lighter in weight than the old wooden horses. There were one or two drawbacks, however.

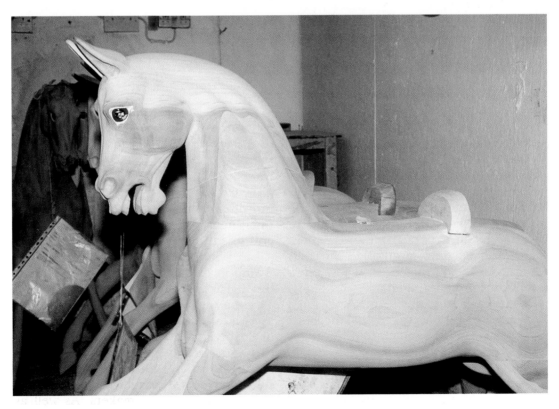

*Stevenson Bros copy of an Ayers horse.*

*Anthony Dew, The Rocking Horse Shop.*

Fibreglass was not cheap, and so there was not much difference in price between this style and a wooden horse. Any accessories had to be pop-riveted on, so replacements had to be removable as damage to the fibreglass was not easy to repair and had to be done by an expert. Another problem was the terrible smell given off by the resin when it was being mixed, so it was not a hobby for the garden shed.

A husband and wife team, A. P. E. S. Rocking Horses, have been making both fibre glass and hand-crafted wooden horses very successfully.

At the end of the century, as at the beginning, the majority of rocking horses were still made of wood, many more than before being made of hardwood instead of the pine and beech of the first half of the century. There were no big manufacturers, except perhaps Merrythought; the industry was very much in the hands of individual craftsmen, which was just what the public wanted. Some of the many craftsmen included Robert Mullis in Wiltshire, White Horses in Welwyn, Richard Ayling in Camarthen; in fact most counties had at least one good quality maker.

Some rocking horses were made simply as a toy, while others were made as an item of beauty and a treasured piece of furniture, such as those made by D. & N. Kiss, another husband and wife team, at the Rocking Horse Workshop in Shropshire.

It was a very fickle trade. During the three months leading up to Christmas the

*Arabian Horse, A. P. E. S. Rocking Horses.*

orders would come rolling in, but the other nine months could be very lean, and for this reason most small firms diversified. Woody White in Cheddar, for example, also taught and made carousel horses and other carvings.

Another type of horse that appeared in the 1980s was the laminated horse. This was made from thick laminations of plywood, this material being readily available, cheaper than good-quality planks of wood, and very strong and stable. New ideas on how to make the body were tried and the best ones adopted. The idea was to be able to see all the swirls that showed off the different colours in the plywood when it was clear varnished, yet still have a good, strong horse, some even big enough for older children. This method was very slow to gain popularity. Relko, taken over later by Haddon Rocking Horses Ltd, was

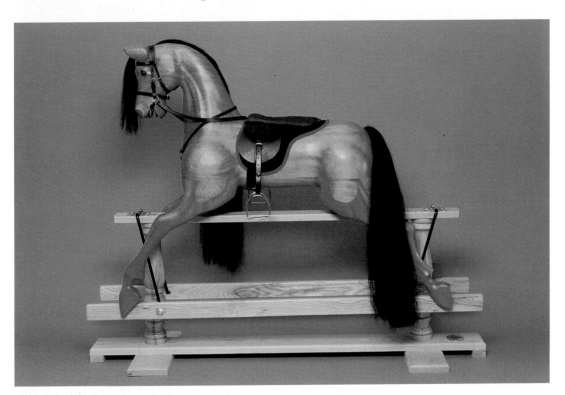

*White Horses.*

*D. & N. Kiss, The Rocking Horse Workshop.*

one of the first, followed by Ian Armstrong and then Judy F. Designs, another maker who also teaches and makes other items.

Another material that was tried right at the end of the century was MDF (medium density fibre), a type of compressed wood fibre which could be cut or carved in any direction using power tools. This made it attractive as a quick way to carve out a horse. It was strong, but had some major drawbacks in that it was heavy and extremely dusty to work with, and the dust could lead to serious infections of the throat and lungs.

Most of the people trading in the last fifteen years of the twentieth century have continued on into the twenty-first century. Countless granddads made a rocking horse as a retirement hobby, then found it so fascinating that they ended up making half a dozen or more. Still more serious makers started up, such as Geoff Martin at

*Haddon Rocking Horses, Relko Range.*

Horsecraft, who specializes in large horses, and Peter Furr of Furzdown Rocking Horses who makes to order.

The one company that crowned them all was Collinson & Sons of Liverpool, which started in 1836 and was a leading manufacturer throughout the twentieth century, until the last Collinson brother sold out in the 1990s. The people who bought the company had no idea about rocking horse making, so the firm finally collapsed. However, one of the sons of the family, who had been making horses all his working life, has started again as Stephen Collinson to take the family name on into the twenty-first century.

There are many more makers of rocking horses throughout Britain and the world than have been mentioned here. All have their own ideas, which makes for an interesting variety in style, quality and price.

Craft Guilds and the British Toy Makers Guild can provide details of good rocking horse makers. The British Toy Makers Guild reports that although they cover all types of toys, 14 per cent of their members are rocking horse makers. In addition, at the last Nuremberg Toy Fair of the twentieth century, the biggest fair of its kind in Europe, there were only two rocking horse makers – both British. If a toy looks and moves remotely like a rocking horse, it is surprising how a child's imagination will fill in the missing details and they will be loved by their owners. There were

15

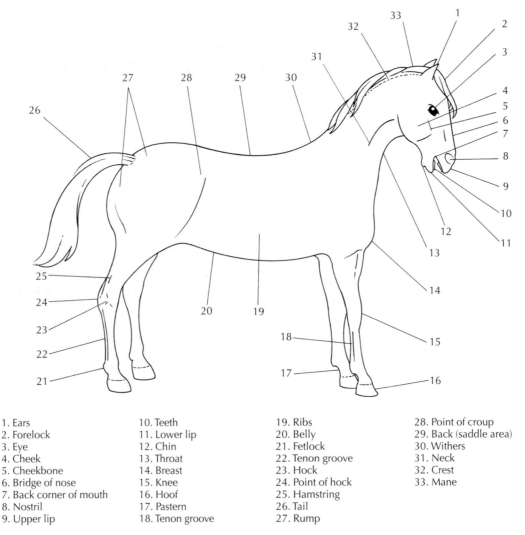

| 1. Ears | 10. Teeth | 19. Ribs | 28. Point of croup |
| 2. Forelock | 11. Lower lip | 20. Belly | 29. Back (saddle area) |
| 3. Eye | 12. Chin | 21. Fetlock | 30. Withers |
| 4. Cheek | 13. Throat | 22. Tenon groove | 31. Neck |
| 5. Cheekbone | 14. Breast | 23. Hock | 32. Crest |
| 6. Bridge of nose | 15. Knee | 24. Point of hock | 33. Mane |
| 7. Back corner of mouth | 16. Hoof | 25. Hamstring | |
| 8. Nostril | 17. Pastern | 26. Tail | |
| 9. Upper lip | 18. Tenon groove | 27. Rump | |

*Points of a horse as used on a rocking horse.*

therefore thousands of rocking horses in use at the end of the twentieth century. The world leader in rocking horse making was Britain, and the enthusiasm to make or own a horse was still very strong, and more widely spread over the population than at the beginning of the century. Are the boom times coming again?

# 2

# DESIGNING A ROCKING HORSE, TOOLS AND WORKSHOP KNOWHOW

## DESIGNING A ROCKING HORSE

A simple rocking horse design suitable for a toddler consists of a cut-out silhouette of a head attached to a plank of wood and four legs on little rockers. There are a few guidelines to follow even for this: all joints should be secure, with no rough edges, and the seat should have a back rest to prevent the toddler from sliding off the end.

The next step is to make something that has the proportions and curves of a horse. Diagram 1 is a guide to the proportions needed, bearing in mind that every horse is slightly different, and that bigger differences occur between breeds. For example, the Shetland pony has little legs, a racing horse has long legs, while a Shire horse is built for strength. The diagram is based on a horse used for riding for pleasure.

Draw a silhouette of a horse (the back of wallpaper is ideal for this as it is big and cheap), using line A on which to base your

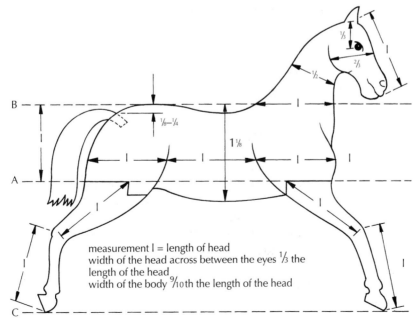

measurement I = length of head
width of the head across between the eyes $\frac{1}{3}$ the length of the head
width of the body $\frac{9}{10}$th the length of the head

*The proportions of a horse.*

measurements, with line B as another guide and line C as the position of the hoof rail or rocker.

Draw the head and neck first. A common fault is to curve the front of the neck round and under the chin, but if you look at a horse, unless its head is stretched out, the jaw/cheek bone cuts round and upwards making a sharp turn in direction

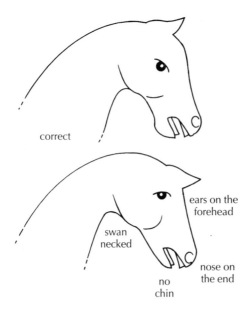

*Position of ears, eyes and neck.*

for the outline. The ears should be on top of the head, not sliding down the forehead.

When satisfied with the head, the other proportions can be added using the head as the unit of measurement. A few attempts may be required to get it right.

Next, decide on the type of wood you are going to use – what sort of grain should it have? – and how you are going to split the horse into manageable pieces for the wood available. The size of the area you have to work in, the tools available to you, the joints to be used and the strength of the finished horse must also be considered.

Following this, make patterns from paper or tracing paper using the master drawing, and then transfer them to cardboard, hardboard or another durable material that will hold its shape and stay flat. The best way to measure a rocking horse is to use the length of the body as all other measurements vary depending on the stance of the horse.

The ears should always be upright, or better still pointing forwards. They should never point backwards, even if you make a horse in a galloping position, as they will be a hazard to riders; should an accident occur, carved ears are hard, not soft like a real horse.

The horse should be balanced on a swinger stand so that it is upright, and the pillars of the stand should be in front and behind the body, but no further out than the hooves. If the horse is on rockers, a slight lean forward is fine, as the rider sits slightly back from the centre which evens up the position of the horse. A slight flattening in the centre of the underside of the rockers (15cm) will help to keep that position while the rider mounts.

Usually the legs of the horse are splayed out at 102.5 degrees from the underside of the body, to give some sideways stability against the rough play of a child.

If the horse is going to be on rockers and you want to keep the pure lines of the horse, mount it on a platform between the rockers, which would be 14cm apart for a 66cm horse at the centre. The pairs of legs do not have to mirror each other, but can be in walking or trotting positions. There is still some degree of restriction on the length of stride because of strain and the distribution of weight.

If the two legs marked X on the diagram opposite are not able to take their full share of the load, while the other two are overloaded; all four are liable to collapse with the constant rocking motion.

*The position of the legs.*

The 102.5-degree angle of the legs has certainly stood the test of time. The legs do crack at the top, but if they have been put in properly it might take 100 years for this to happen.

If you want to have a bent leg, as in Chapter 9, where the grain of the wood is interrupted, do this in two slices with the grain going in different directions. Glue the two halves together, which makes it hard for the leg to split along any of the grain. Legs should always be made of something that can take the strain, such as hardwood or thick, good-quality plywood.

Thick, good-quality softwood can be used but it is not the best.

The boat-shaped rockers of the old Georgian-style horses are aesthetically beautiful, as the horse is at full gallop with all four legs outstretched. The rockers sweep inwards towards the ends, which curve up high into a curl. The horse itself is nearer to the ground than later horses, being low slung between the rockers for stability, but its two main drawbacks are that the horse can be rocked so vigorously that it can throw the rider – usually over the head – and that

*Modern bow rocker on left; nineteenth-century rocker on right.*

19

the strain on the tops of the legs is such that even with the front legs positioned differently, they crack out.

With a swinger stand the horse is much more stable as it can only rock as far as the bars will swing. It is still important to keep the centre of gravity low, so the belly of the horse should not be more than 30–60mm (depending on size) above the top rail of the stand. The hoof rail should be no higher than a third of the way up the height of the completed stand.

The rockers are cut with the longest grain in the centre. If they are so long that the grain at the ends is very short (bear in mind that children will stand on the ends to get a ride), each rocker must be made in two halves and joined in the middle, with an extra piece of wood screwed or bolted over this joint on the inside. The joint is usually disguised by a platform on top, thus adding more weight and stability where it is needed.

The head can be tried in different positions, for example a turned head (see Chapter 9). If a forward position is used, as if the horse is racing, and it is mounted on rockers, make sure they are long enough and can accommodate all the weight bearing down on the front. You might need an extra thickness of wood at the rump end as a counter-balance. The front legs of a racing horse start from a different position on the body.

Beware of stretching the back legs too far, as after a certain point a horse will bend its legs rather than have a longer stride, for example when coming down a hill.

Offer the whole horse up (screwed together if you feel it necessary) to see if the design works before making anything permanent by gluing.

Incorporating springs into the stand could be interesting, but the inventions so far have either rusted out or suffered from metal fatigue. Perhaps there is a new concept waiting to be invented…

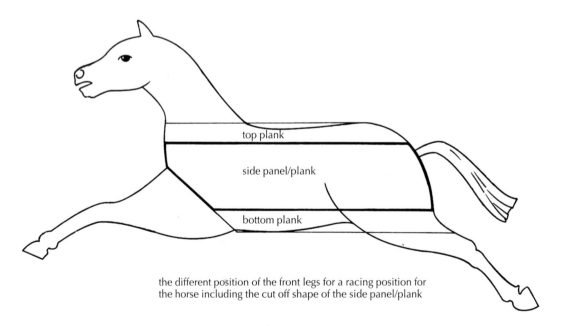

the different position of the front legs for a racing position for the horse including the cut off shape of the side panel/plank

*The position of the front legs of a racing horse, including the cut-out shape of the side panel/plank.*

## A SAMPLE DESIGN

This design incorporates a foam-padded backrest covered with leather cloth, for those children with a balance or back problem. This is removable so the horse can also be used in the conventional way.

The gaps in the sides of the horse are to enable a harness to be put on if necessary. The horse in the photograph overleaf was made for a docile child; for a very active child, struts may be needed at the back to give extra strength. The horse has a traditional saddle because the foam pad can come right down against the wooden back rest, making it the bottom of the extended back rest. The frame is attached to the hoof rails by two bolts with wing nuts, the wings of the nuts being on the inside of the hoof rail.

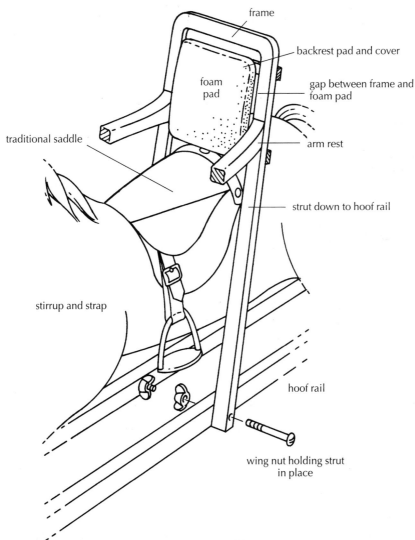

*The high back of the seat for children with back problems.*

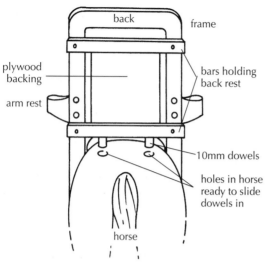

*Back view of high backrest showing position of dowels to help support the frame.*

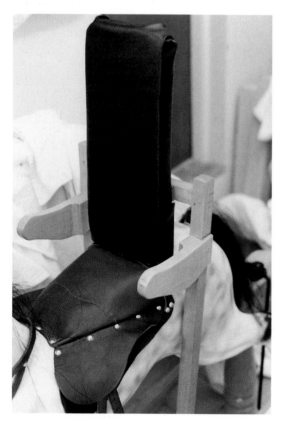

*High backrest for a child with back and balance problems.*

## Materials

- 25–30mm thick beech for the frame
- 2.5cm thick pad of medium-density foam with cover
- 2 × 10mm dowels, length as required
- 2 × bolts with wing nuts, length as required
- Various No. 8 countersink screws

The instructions are not complete as each back rest depends on the child's size and capability, and the size of the horse, so this is the start of a design to do for yourself.

# TOOLS

Other than the tools commonly found in the toolbox of a DIY enthusiast, only a few specialist tools are required when making a rocking horse. Different tools are used on different horses, as outlined below.

- Bandsaw to cut out the pieces of the horse
- Jigsaw to cut large pieces of plywood
- Drill on a stand to make vertical holes; the drill can also double up as a hand drill
- Rubber-backed disc for the hand drill, on which to attach sanding discs of different grades
- Morticer used only for the two plywood horses: the Plywood Filly and the Push-me Pull-me Horse
- Clamps of varying sizes
- Gouges of 13mm and 25mm–38mm
- Chisels – sizes as for gouges
- Sharpening stones for above
- Round or square mallet; both are effective
- Surform, both round and half round
- Spirit level, set square and protractor
- Plane or planer. Used on horses with hollow middles, and for the bottom of heads if the wood is not already prepared

- Rifler files for wood. These are of various shapes to enable you to get to awkward places
- Vice, large enough to hold parts of the horse while working on them, for example legs and head
- Angle grinder with attachments. One attachment has teeth that look like those of a chainsaw, and is just as lethal. It is used to cut surplus wood off horses (not plywood horses) and needs to be used with great care.

  Another attachment, which is not so lethal, is for sanding discs. A coarse disc is very good for shaping plywood
- Power file

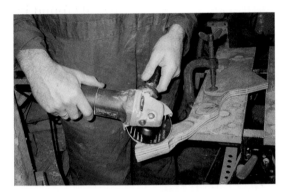

*Using an angle grinder with a sanding attachment to sand plywood.*

# WORKSHOP KNOWHOW

This section is mainly for the amateur rocking horse maker. Most professionals will be familiar with the tips provided.

## PLANNING YOUR WORKSPACE

(1) A tin of sealer left on the window sill with the lid not quite closed will become an unusable jelly before it is half used, sometimes within hours. Paints do not fair much better. The coldest place you have is the best, usually under the work bench.

(2) Powders used to make such things as glue and gesso need to be stored in a dry place, for example a shelf up near the roof.

(3) To avoid a pot of glue or a small tin of paint being tipped over, put each into a larger empty tin with pebbles (no sand) or old nails and screws in the bottom to use as ballast.

(4) All machinery that is not hand-held should be carefully placed so that there is no wobble. If it is moved, it should be rechecked before use, even if you are in a hurry. Wobbly equipment causes accidents and poor workmanship.

(5) As well as caring for your chisels and gouges, keep them where the tips of their blades will not get damaged or go rusty.

*Power file.*

*The clutter of a working bench and the tools at hand.*

The same applies to your saws, which are often forgotten but need their blades kept sharp too.

## CARING FOR WOOD

(1) If planks of wood are stored for any length of time outside or under cover without heating, spaces should be left between the planks and the ends painted so that they can dry (or dampen) at an even rate along the plank. This reduces splitting.
(2) Clamp together any wood that you have cut to size for stand and body if you are not using it immediately. This helps to avoid warping.
(3) Another way to stop bowing across the grain, especially with softwood, is to look at the end of the plank where the cross section shows the growth rings (if the wood is thick enough). Use the wood so that the outside growth ring is on the outside of your work as this can avoid gaping seams.

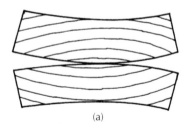

(a)

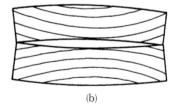

(b)

(a) warping caused by shrinkage leaving gaps between the two planks
(b) turn them over and the growth rings have the core of hartwood on the outside. The warping is reduced

*End view of planks.*

## SCREWS AND NAILS

(1) Clean out the slot of an old screw with an old hacksaw blade or fine jigsaw blade before attempting to unscrew it.
(2) To undo a tight screw, give it a half turn tighter and then undo it. If it still won't move, heat the top then twist it, or give it a good tap with a hammer.
(3) Lift out a nail or tack by putting the end of a flat screwdriver under the head and giving it a half turn. When working on rocking horses, put it under the nail and the leather, cloth or whatever you are using, to loosen them all.
(4) The size of a pilot hole should be no bigger than the shaft of the screw without the thread.
(5) When screwing two pieces of wood together that are neither clamped nor glued, always put a hole through the first piece of wood that is larger in diameter than the screw, and a short pilot hole into the second piece of wood, or the screw may not bite into the second piece and you will end up screwing the two pieces apart.

## PAINT PROBLEMS

(1) Pouring boiling water over a cintride disc will loosen resin and hard-packed saw-dust. This will not work if paint has clogged the disc; if this is the case it will need soaking in brush cleaner.
(2) Soap and cold running water can sometimes take out the paint that stays in the top of the paint brush and clogs up the hairs, even after a swill in brush cleaner. This leaves the brush pliable right up to the top.
(3) Do not be tempted to use the same brush for different colours as there is always some paint left which seeps down into the bristles, and you could leave black streaks on a lovely coat of white.

24

## MAKING THE ROCKING HORSE

(1) Rub a glass eyeball in the palm of your hand just before setting it into the eye socket. There is usually just enough natural grease on your hand to leave a thin layer of grease on the eyeball, so that when it has dried in the socket and the head is being painted, you can paint straight over the eye as well. When the paint is thoroughly dry, scribe round the paint at the edge of the eyeball with the point of a sharp knife and it will peel off the eye leaving the rest untouched.

(2) Plastic wood filler used for setting the eyes hardens very quickly in warm, dry weather, but takes much longer in cold, damp weather. On warm days, make the setting of eyes the first priority in the morning when it is still cool, giving you those extra few minutes to make the eyes and lids (where appropriate).

(3) If the plastic wood filler is very sticky, dip your knife blade in water so that the filler will not adhere to it.

(4) Clean brasses such as rosettes by smearing them with ketchup and leaving them overnight. Rinse in water in the morning and all the grime will be gone, even from the corners which cannot be reached by conventional methods. This method does not remove paint, however. Soaking the brasses in Coca-Cola is another method that can be used.

(5) When using machinery, ear protectors are a must, as is a mask. Two more items that are sometimes forgotten are a tie back for long hair and protective glasses. Also beware of loose clothing.

(6) Round off the tenon edge that is going into the mortice, or a dowel going into a hole, with sanding paper so the edge does not foul against the side of the mortice or the hole.

(7) If more than one dowel is being put into a joint where there is likely to be stress on the joint, such as the leg to body joint or head to body joint, put them in at different angles so that stresses will be counteracted.

# — 3 —

# ACCESSORIES

## TOOLS

- Hammer for nailed-on saddle and bridle
- Rivet punch (only used if you have removable tack; the reins are riveted together)
- Leather punch for rivet holes on bridle and stirrups
- Knife for cutting leather
- Stitch wheel for marking the length of stitches
- Awl for piercing the stitch marks
- Two leather needles with blunt ends for stitching leather
- Beeswax for thread lubrication
- Edging tool to score an even line along strapping

As materials differ depending on the size and type of the horse, the quantities quoted within this chapter are for a 66cm Medium Standard Horse. Dome nails are used as they are safer; it is harder to be scratched by them. Finally, as discussed on page 6, all leather must be vegetable-tanned.

## THE SADDLE

The easiest saddle design is a piece of leather or leather cloth shaped like a saddle and nailed on to the back of the horse, without any padding.

## SIMPLE SADDLE

*Materials*
- 60cm × 37.5cm piece of leather, 2–3mm thick and very pliable
- 2 × 25mm solid 'D' rings
- Padding for the seat
- 30 nails, usually brass-domed
- 6 × 25mm nails
- 2m thread
- 17.5mm × 2.5mm length of webbing or strong strapping

(1) Cut out two pieces of saddle-shaped leather, the larger piece 42cm × 25cm, the smaller piece 25cm × 23cm. See the diagram opposite.
(2) Loop the webbing through the 'D' rings and lay it across the larger piece of leather, 4.5cm from the front edge nearest the neck. Loop the ends of the webbing back on themselves to above the line of the seat, with a 'D' ring held within the loop on each side.
(3) Holding the webbing and rings in place, mark the seat on the top piece with a stitch wheel and lay it on top of the bottom piece.
(4) Sew the two pieces together around the seat, including the webbing where it is laid over the stitch line. Leave room to push in the padding before completing the stitching.
(5) Nail the saddle to the horse along the stitch line.

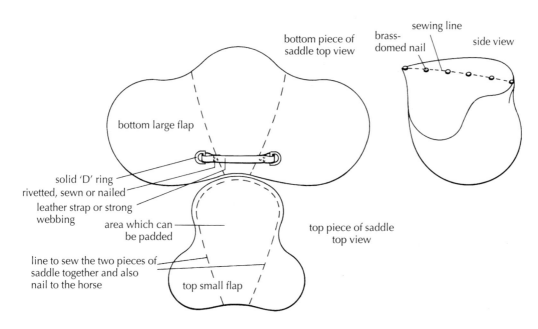

*A simple saddle.*

*Nailed-on tack with a simple saddle.*

## TRADITIONAL SADDLE

This is a copy of the nineteenth-century rocking horse saddle, when there was a wooden back rest or cantle to keep the seat sloping forward. It was used almost universally up to the middle of the twentieth century, and can still be found on many new horses. *See* Chapter 4 for details of inserting the wooden back rest.

*Materials*
- 60cm × 37.5cm piece of leather, 2–3mm thick and very pliable
- A matching piece of leather, the length of the back rest and 25mm wide
- 22cm long piece of cloth which is as wide as the widest part of the seat plus 50mm (muslin can be used as it is only to stop the padding pushing out)
- 30–40 × brass-domed nails
- 2m thread
- Fire-retardant foam 25mm thick, shaped to fit and thinner at neck end

(1) The size of the saddle varies a great deal from horse to horse. The main measurements required are: straight down the back of the horse from the back rest to the neck; across from side to side over the back rest for the seat.
(2) The leather seat should be triangular in shape, with the point at the neck cut off. The flaps on each side are cut out separately, and the cloth is cut at least 25mm larger than the seat of the saddle. The small flaps should be long enough to cover the buckles of the stirrup straps.
(3) Using a stitch marker, mark round the edge of the seat. Put the padding in place with the cloth underneath, the leather seat over the top and the flaps at each side, then sew around the edge of the seat area through the entire thickness.
(4) Nail the saddle to the horse just below the stitch line along the sides of the seat, and nail a 25mm wide strip of leather along the top of the back rest with the back edge of the saddle seat underneath it.

## SOFT REMOVABLE SADDLE

*Materials (for small/medium horse, 260mm long)*
- 65cm × 50cm piece of vegetable-tanned panel hide
- 2m waxed linen thread
- 2 × leather needles
- 82cm strapping for girth (webbing preferred)
- 1 × iroko buckle, or its equivalent, and tip.
- 3 × eyelets
- 2 × brass screws with round heads that only just clear the middle of the eyelets
- 26cm × 20cm × 15cm block of high-density fire retardent foam
- 2 × 25mm brass 'D' rings
- 300mm × 25mm length of trapping for the 'D' rings

*Tip*
If you are not sure what to do, try making the saddle using material first to become familiar with the sequence (the material does not have to be new).

(1) Cut out then mark all the pieces with an edging tool, following the lines on the plans.
(2) Use the template to mark the inner lines of the saddle base, making sure all centre lines match up.
(3) Using a stitch marker wheel, mark the lines, working from the centre line outwards each time, for the top piece, front gusset and bottom piece. Punch each hole with an awl where the stitch marker has indicated. For the back gusset, use the outer top line as a guide when marking the inner wide line.
(4) Starting in the centre at the top, stitch mark the outer line in the same way as the one line at the bottom.

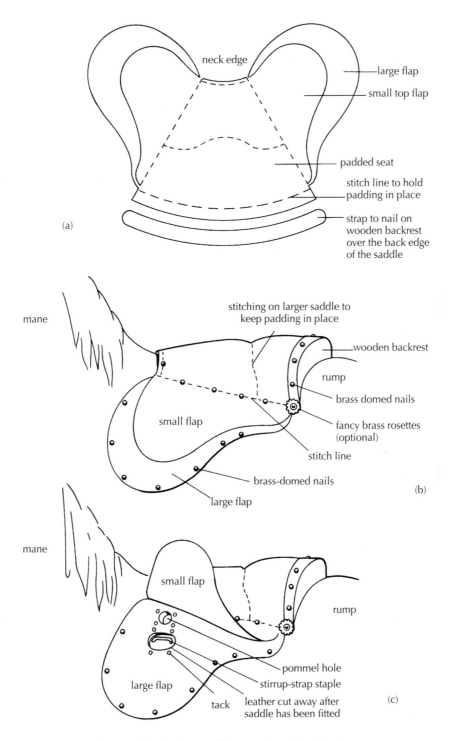

*The traditional saddle with a wooden back rest: (a) top view; (b) side view; (c) side view with small top flap lifted.*

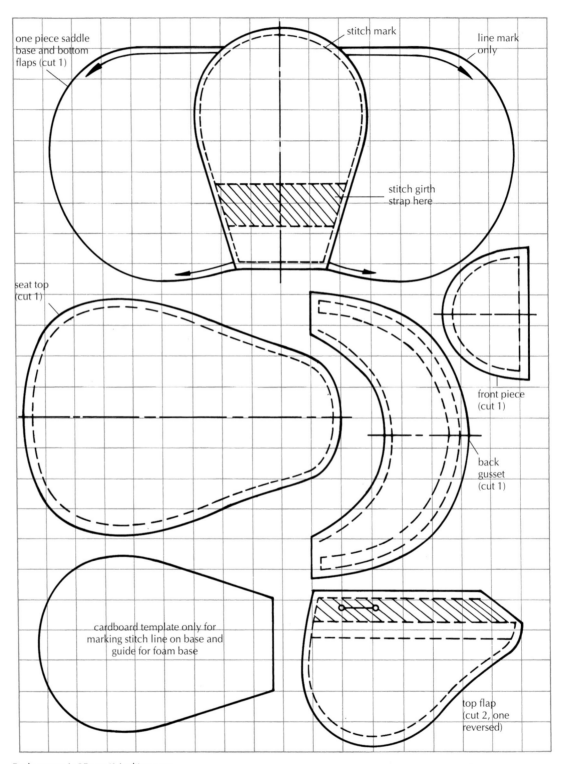

one piece saddle base and bottom flaps (cut 1)

stitch mark

line mark only

stitch girth strap here

seat top (cut 1)

front piece (cut 1)

back gusset (cut 1)

cardboard template only for marking stitch line on base and guide for foam base

top flap (cut 2, one reversed)

Each square is 25mm (1 inch) square

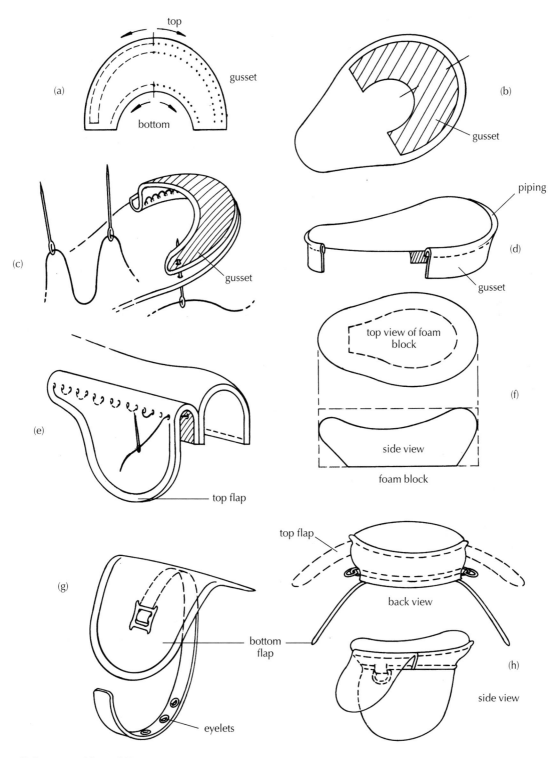

*Soft removable saddle instructions.*

(5) Using an awl punch, stitch holes on the top outer edge, then one to match on the inner marked line. It is important to have the same amount of stitches in each row and for each row to end up where the edges are marked (fig. a). The inner stitch holes will be closer together to allow for the curve of the line.

(6) Place the back gusset face to face with the top back so the centre lines are matching and the gusset is suede side up (fig. b).

(7) Starting at the centre line hole and using two needles, double sew by hand through the three holes so that the gusset is sewn tightly back on itself (fig. c). Do the same in the other direction for the other half. Match the front gusset to the centre front line and stitch in the same way. Turn the whole piece right side out and you will have a piping effect (fig. d).

(8) Punch holes in the flaps, making sure the two parallel lines match up. Fold the flaps over on to themselves (fig. e).

(9) Sew either side of the saddle top, matching front to front gusset and stitching the parallel lines straight through to the top piece (the bottom line of holes is to be sewn to the base piece).

(10) Cut out a piece of high-density foam to fit the shape of the seat (fig. f) (an electric carving knife is good for this). A cardboard base template is useful here to mark the angle to be cut away for the bottom of the block.

(11) Using a machine, or by hand, sew the girth buckle on to the girth, and the girth strap to the base piece (see plans). Heavy-weight webbing is most commonly used for this, however strong leather can also be used. The buckle needs to be on the left side of the horse so the shorter part of the strap is on this side under the flap (fig. g). The 'D' rings for the stirrup straps are joined by one long piece of leather or webbing so that they can protrude from either side of the saddle seat and can be included in the stitching of the base to the top (fig. h). It is recommended that the girth incorporate eyelet holes which clip on to dome-headed screws that are left 2mm proud of the underside of the horse, for added safety against slippage.

# STIRRUP STRAPS

*Materials*
- 120cm × 12–20mm × 3mm very strong piece of leather
- 2 × buckles to match the width of the strapping (12–20mm)
- 4 × rivets or sewing thread
- 2 × custom-made staples

**Method One**

(1) Attach a stirrup to each end of the strapping, looping an end through the top of the stirrup and stitching or riveting the loop.

(2) Screw (with a cup) the centre of the strap to the centre of the horse's back, just below the neck.

(3) Nail the saddle on top.

The disadvantage with this method is that there is no adjustment for a growing child.

**Method Two**

(1) Gouge out a slot 25mm high, 38mm wide and 16mm deep, each side 25mm lower than the straight line of the saddle seat, but far enough forward so that it will be covered by the small saddle flap (see Diagram 9). In this depression, hammer in a U-shaped staple under the large saddle flap, leaving a gap of 16mm behind it; this will be covered by the small flap. The staples are made of 3mm heavy duty, stiff wire, and are 19mm wide at the bottom of the U with two 32mm long prongs.

(2) Cut a hole around the staple in the large flap, securing the edges with small tacks. Fold the 120cm strap in half, sew or rivet a buckle on one end of each piece

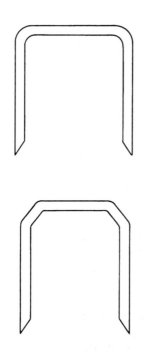

*Stirrup-strap staples.*

The 'U' staple is not needed for removable saddles and simple saddles, as the stirrup strap is threaded through the 'D' ring attached to the saddle.

# CRUPPER

*Materials*
- 1 × piece of 12mm strapping, 22–38cm long
- 4–10 × brass-domed nails.

The crupper strap is for decoration only on a rocking horse.

(1) Nail one end behind the back rest or saddle, then loop round the horse's tail and return to the same spot behind the saddle, nailing intermittently with brass-domed nails along its length; with a simple saddle this can be stiched into the back.

and punch a line of holes at the other end.
(3) Put the end through the stirrup then loop round the 'U' staple and buckle to make an adjustable stirrup strap.

# MARTINGALE

*Materials*
- 1 × piece of 13–20mm strapping, approximately 100cm long

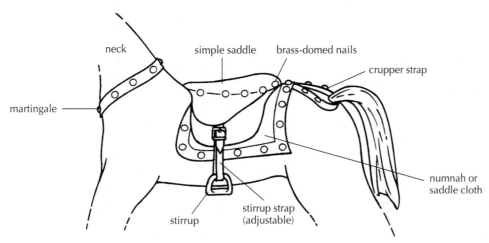

*Details of harness for a rocking horse.*

- 10 × brass-domed nails; or for a removable martingale: 1 extra length of strapping, 4 × rivets, 1 × 20 or 25mm 'D' ring and 1 × buckle the same width as the strapping

Again, the martingale is for decoration only.

(1) Using brass nails, nail the martingale around the base of the neck, ending in a 'V' in the middle of the breast. From here, take a piece of strapping down between the horse's front legs and fasten it off with a hidden nail. The centre of the V is a good place for a ribbon or brass rosette.
(2) If the martingale is removable, do not nail it to the horse. Where the three ends of strapping meet on the breast, loop them round the 'D' ring and sew or rivet. Also, make a loop on the end that passes under the horse so that the girth strap of a removable saddle can go through it. This can be buckled for adjustment.

# NUMNAH

*Materials*
- 50cm × 30cm of material
- 2m of decorative border
- sewing cotton
- 20 × brass nails

As for the crupper and martingale, this is for decoration only, but it does provide a chance to add some colour to a horse. Fire-retardent upholstery velvet is good for this.

(1) The numnah fits across the back of the horse, under the saddle, between the withers and croup, and extends down each side of the body to below the large flap of the saddle.
(2) The lower corners should be rounded at the front, extending to a point towards the rear of the horse. It is not very practical for use with a removable saddle as it will slip about when the child is trying to saddle up.

# BRIDLE

The bridles included here are the common British style, but they can be adapted for many other styles.

*Tip*
Nail the mane on to the horse before making the bridle so the bridle can be made to go across the head, over the join where the mane meets the forelock.

## NAIL-ON BRIDLE

This has been the most popular version of the bridle over the last 200 years, and uses a bit.

*Materials*
- 1 × piece of 13mm strapping, 100cm long
- 16 × brass-domed nails

(1) Nail a piece of strapping above the back corner of the mouth and take it over the bridge of the nose, round behind the chin and under the jaw to the beginning. Butt the two ends, then nail them down. This is the nose band.
(2) Loop one end of the strapping through the ring of the bit then loop it back on itself. Nail it above the mouth. Extend the strapping up the cheek, over the head behind the ears, over the point at which the mane and forelock meet, and down the other cheek. Loop through the other ring of the bit and nail just above the mouth. Also nail halfway up the cheek and at the temple. This is the head strap.
(3) For the brow band, stretch a piece of strapping under the forelock and just

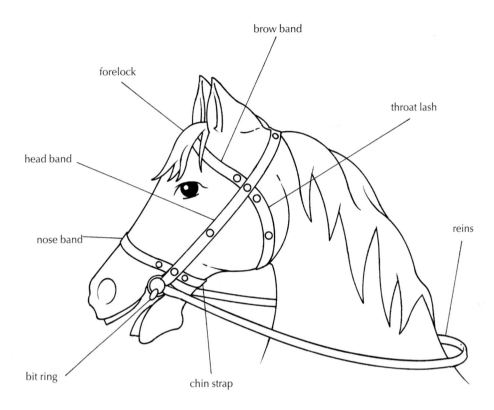

*A traditional nailed-on bridle.*

below the ears from one temple to the other, butting and nailing the ends to the head strap at the temple. The throat lash goes from the same temple point under the jaw to the other temple. The temple is a favourite place for decorative brass or ribbon rosettes; this also covers up the ends of all the straps.

## CLOSED-MOUTH BRIDLE

This bridle is suitable for a horse with a closed mouth.

*Materials*
- 1 × piece of 13mm strapping, 100cm long
- 16 × brass-domed nails
- 2 × screw eyelets

(1) Follow the instructions for the nail-on bridle. The head band is butted and nailed touching the nose band in line with the mouth. Just below, and through the actual nose band strapping at the back corner of the mouth, insert a screw eyelet on each side, to which the reins will be attached.

## REMOVABLE BRIDLE

*Materials*
- 1 × 58cm × 25mm strap; 1 × 30cm × 16mm strap; and 1 × 38cm × 12mm strap
- a minimum of 10 rivets or sewing thread
- 3 × 12mm buckles

(1) The 58cm × 25mm strap is used for the head strap and goes from the bit ring

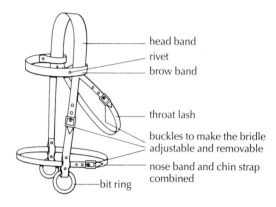

head band
rivet
brow band

throat lash

buckles to make the bridle
adjustable and removable

nose band and chin strap
combined

bit ring

*A removable and adjustable bridle.*

on one side of the mouth, up and over the head where the mane is joined to the fore-lock, behind the ears and down the other side of the face to the other ring. Allow 7cm turn back at each end, plus an extra 6.5cm on the side that goes down the left cheek (left is defined as that which would be the horse's left). Split this strap equally in half along its width, from its ends up as far as the temples on both sides, including the extra 6.5cm on the left side. This makes two smaller straps of approximately 12mm wide going down each cheek. The ends of the front straps on either side go through the bit rings and turn back on themselves by 7cm.

(2) On the right strap, make a fastening close to the bit, either using a rivet or by sewing, and another fastening approximately 38mm further up the strap, so that there is an opening between the two fastening points.

(3) Rivet or sew a buckle on one end of the 38cm × 12mm strap, and punch a row of holes in the other end, then thread the strap through the opening created in (2) so that it can be fitted round the nose and fastened by the buckle underneath, behind the chin. This makes the nose band removable and adjustable.

(4) There should be plenty of slack on the front strap going up the left cheek; cut this through about halfway up the cheek and rivet or sew a 12mm buckle on the lower end, then punch a row of holes in the upper end to make the vertical head band adjustable and removable.

(5) Tuck the free 10mm back strap coming down the right cheek under the throat, then cut it and put a buckle on the end. Punch a row of holes in the end of the corresponding back strap coming down the left cheek, and buckle it to the one from the right side, making the throat lash. For convenience, the throat lash may need cutting shorter.

(6) To make the brow band, loop one end of the 30cm × 16mm length of strapping round the head strap at the temple on one side, and back on itself to be riveted or sewn (leaving the head band free moving).The brow band goes across the fore-head under the forelock and is looped around the head band, leaving it free for final adjustments. A rosette can be added to the brow band. All buckles should be on the left side.

It is suggested that an adjustable bridle is not used on a very small horse as it makes the face too cluttered; a simple nail-on bri-dle looks much better.

# BIT

Heavy duty galvanized wire, the width of the mouth plus enough to make a loop to take a 25mm ring each end, makes a sim-ple bit. As the ends of the wire loop and the rings are the only parts to be seen clearly, this is usually enough. Other types of rocking horse bit can be bought.

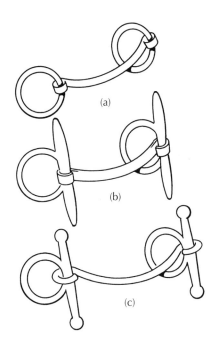

*Traditional bits: (a) a simple hand-forged type bit, as used in the early nineteenth century; (b) a hand-forged bit like this one was used in the late nineteenth and early twentieth century on better-quality horses ; (c) this type of bit is typical of those used by Triang in the mid-twentieth century and is still available.*

# REINS

Rocking horse reins are kept short, as most non-riders hold the reins at full length so they sit too far back in the saddle.

*Materials*
- 76cm × 12mm × 3mm length of robust leather strapping
- 2 × swivel clips or 4 × rivets or sewing thread

(1) Loop the ends of the strapping round the rings of the bit and rivet or sew them together. Alternatively, put a swivel clip on each end, which is fun to use and takes the wear away from the vulnerable spot on the reins – where the strap goes through the rings.

# STIRRUPS

The measurement across the sole of the shoe is the size of the stirrup. However, unless a blacksmith is available, you should not attempt to make stirrups. All sizes of stirrups for children can be bought. Real horse stirrups should not be used as these are too large and have sharp bases for boot grip.

# MANE AND TAIL

*Materials*
- Even after 200 years, the best material for manes and tails is still horse hair. Other products have been tried but are not so durable, and of course horse hair is appropriate.

*Mane*
There are three common methods of attaching the hair to a rocking horse's head and neck.

**Method One**
(1) The traditional method is to use hair that is still on the hide of a pony's or horse's tail; the skin has been cured to become hide and the hair is still attached to it. The hide is very stiff and will need soaking overnight in cold water before it becomes pliable enough to cut with a sharp knife into 13–20mm wide strips. Cut from the hide side to protect the hair from being cut as well.
(2) After the horse has been painted or varnished and before the bridle is put on, nail the strips on to the back of the head

and neck with 25mm round wire nails, butting the joins down the neck and hiding the heads of the nails by hammering them well into the hair without splitting the hide.

(3) Finish the mane about 50–75mm above the bottom of the neck so it does not bunch at the bottom and get in the way of the stirrups and rider. Turn one short strip round so the hair is laying in the opposite direction, nail it between the ears and also butt it to the rest of the mane just behind the ears. This makes a forelock.

### Tip

To avoid shedding hair, do not comb or brush the hair until the hide of the tail is completely dry, which can be a few days.

### Method Two

(1) The second method involves the use of loose hair. This should be long – 50mm or more – and should be sewn along the centre to a strip of material or leather, then glued and nailed to the horse's neck. If combings from horses are used they must be thoroughly cleaned as glue does not stick to grease. They should not be used for horses that are to be sold, as the authorities only like professionally cured hides or hair.

### Method Three

(1) A method with which to attach shorter hair – under 30mm long. Glue and clamp one end between two pieces of semi-stiff material such as leather cloth. Nail this to the bottom of a 15mm wide by 25mm deep slot which starts from behind the

ears and goes to within 76mm of the bottom of the neck.

(2) Put another layer of glue in the slot between the hair and the sides of the slot; any space left can be filled with slivers of wood or wood filler. Pull the first 10mm of hair forward between the ears to make the forelock and hold it in place with the bridle head strap.

### Tail

Tail holes and therefore the thickness of tails vary from horse to horse. There are two methods of making a tail.

### Method One

(1) To make a tail from loose hair, thoroughly glue and bind one end of the hair to a 38mm plug with a 4mm diameter hole through its length. Apply the glue and hair in layers until they fill the diameter of the hole. Leave to dry thoroughly; it may take a few days until the glued end (plug) is very stiff.

(2) When ready, smear more glue on the plug, push it as far as possible into the hole, put a screw or nail (60mm × No. 6) in the hole in the centre plug and screw or hammer it home. Wipe away any surplus glue and leave to dry thoroughly.

### Method Two

(1) Attach a piece of the hair on the hide used for the mane to a loosely fitting wooden plug with large tacks. The whole plug and hair should be well glued.

(2) Tap the plug into the tail hole carefully with a mallet, until held solid. The wooden plug should stick out by about 12mm to give the tail 'lift'.

# 4

# MEDIUM STANDARD ROCKING HORSE: THE HORSE

There is nothing difficult about assembling a rocking horse; simple joints are used so that anyone with a working knowledge of carpentry and tools can do it. The skill and interest is in turning the blocks of wood into a three-dimensional horse and stand. A plan which when made up gives a good silhouette helps enormously, as nearly all the proportions are already determined. Actually turning this into what is in one's mind's eye is fascinating, and often becomes an all-consuming hobby. The wonderful thing is that it can be done to whatever degree the maker wishes and that the type of wood will allow – from a very fine sculpture to simply rounding off the edges. There is always the same satisfaction of completion. A child's imagination can always fill in any missing details, and whatever the finish you can be sure it will be loved.

*A Medium Standard Horse.*

Most children adore rocking horses. There is something fundamental about the actual rocking movement; watch a child's face when it is having a ride – they always look happy.

The medium-sized rocking horse is by far the most popular, as unlike the Filly (*see* Chapter 6), which is too small by the time a child reaches the age of five or six, it is big enough to last a child until they are about ten or twelve years old, yet without being so big that it takes up a large proportion of an average-sized room. It is because of its popularity that I have chosen the medium-sized horse (in this case 66cm from chest to rump) on which to describe details of carving and assembly.

The instructions given in Chapters 4 and 5 are for a fully carved horse on a swinger stand, which is the style of horse most people think of when they talk of rocking horses from their childhood. In addition, extra detailed carving is covered in Chapter 9. Bow rockers and other alternative methods and styles of making the horse are included where applicable so that the rocking horse can truly be called your own creation. The appearance follows the lines of a real horse as closely as the wood will allow.

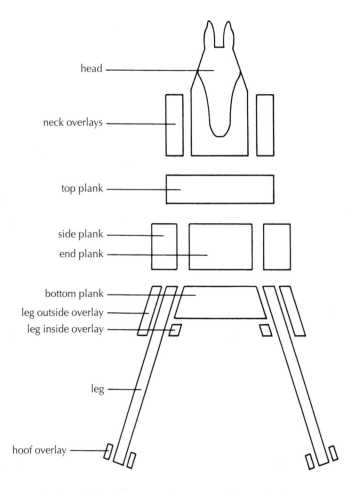

head

neck overlays

top plank

side plank
end plank

bottom plank
leg outside overlay
leg inside overlay

leg

hoof overlay

*Medium Standard Rocking Horse sections viewed from the front.*

The fact that the horse will receive a great deal of hard wear from an unlimited number of children has been taken into consideration in the design. It is also the type of horse a child would find fun to own and with which they could invent countless games to play. Indeed, a rocking horse is an ideal toy for an only child as it becomes a companion in play, with more 'life' than a stuffed toy because it has movement.

The large horse can also be carved and assembled using these instructions for the majority of the work. Use the charts in Chapters 4 and 5 to find the actual sizes, and see also the extra instructions given in Chapter 11.

Before buying the wood and making the horse, as well as deciding on the preferred size, you should also decide on the type of stand required. Points in favour of the two main types are discussed in Chapter 5. All rockers in this book are designed to slide at the end of their rock and not to tip.

**Dimensions:** on a swinger stand, the overall height of the horse from the floor is 110cm; 84cm to the saddle; 66cm breast to rump. The overall width including stand is 43cm and the length is approximately 137cm. On a bow rocker, the overall height from the floor is 102cm; 76cm to the saddle; 66cm from breast to rump. The overall width including rockers is 39cm and the length is approximately 183cm.
**Time taken:** over 50 hours, not including time taken for the glue and paint to dry.

# TOOLS

It is assumed that the person making the rocking horse knows the correct way to handle tools and has a certain amount of woodworking skills, but is not necessarily an expert at either carpentry or carving.

See Chapter 2 for a guide to the basic tools required. It depends on how many horses you are making as to which extra tools it may be worth buying.

- 1 × 28mm countersink bit
- 1 each × 13mm, 9mm, 6mm, 5mm, 3mm drills

# MATERIALS

The softwood referred to is good-quality pine, the same material most old horses were made from, although other woods can be used. One such wood is European lime, as shown in some of the photographs.

- Head: 1 × 430mm × 270mm × 80–90mm piece of softwood
- Top plank :1 × 660mm × 220mm × 50mm softwood plank
- Side planks: 2 × 660mm × 130mm × 50mm softwood planks
- End planks: 2 × 120mm × 130mm × 50mm softwood planks
- Bottom plank: 1 × 660mm × 220mm × 50mm softwood plank
- Front legs: 2 × 32mm thick pieces of hardwood
- Back legs: 2 × 32mm thick pieces of hardwood
- Neck overlay: 2 × 200mm × 160mm × 25mm softwood planks
- Front leg overlay: 2 × 130mm × 90mm × 13mm softwood planks
- Back leg overlay: 2 × 100mm × 90mm × 13mm softwood planks
- 1 × 180cm long × 9mm diameter dowel
- 8 × 6mm × No. 8 and 4 × 7.5mm × No. 10 screws
- 4 × M6 roofing bolts, length to be checked on the finished horse
- 2 × brown glass eyes, 25mm in diameter

*How reclaimed timber can make a good horse (pine).*

## MEDIUM HEAD

The head can be constructed from one piece of good-quality, well-seasoned softwood (*see* Materials, page 41). Alternatively, if a solid piece of timber is not available, the same effect may be obtained by planing and gluing together two 430mm × 270mm × 45mm pieces of wood.

*Tip*
Drawings and photographs of horses' heads will prove useful as they will remind you of the relationship of the features on the head: the eyes, nose, nostrils, mouth and ears. *See* the diagram on page 17.

(1) Drill out the back corner of the mouth vertically with a 13mm twist drill. Then drill a small 8mm hole vertically through the head to mark where the centre of the eyes will be. This also acts as a guide for cutting a hole 6mm deep and 28mm in diameter (3mm larger than the 25mm eye used) with a spade drill. This allows the 'eye' to be seen at all stages of the carving and helps to get the other features in balance.

(2) Cut out the silhouette of the head using a bandsaw.

(3) Using a pencil, draw in the more precise lines of the head, the position of the cheek, and so on, copying the suggested lines shown on the plans. Using a flexible tape rule, draw a pencil line up the centre of the back of the neck, over the ears and down the centre of the face, through the mouth, over the chin, ending at the bottom of the neck. This line can be used to check that each side is even when carving.

(4) The cheek of a horse is very large and flat, so round off all the edges towards the

neck crease and under the throat. The edge nearest the mouth slopes quite abruptly, however, so by the time the slope reaches the back of the mouth it is at least 13mm smaller in width than before carving – 6.7cm or less.

*Tip*
If you have never done any carving before, use an odd piece of softwood and have a dummy run, then any major mistakes will not be expensive and you will be able to tackle the head with more confidence. You might find you also end up with an interesting door stop!

(5) There is another slope inward at the top end of the cheek towards the back of the head, behind the ears, and again above the eyebrows to the base of the ears, so that the thickness of the wood just below the ears is about 6.3cm.

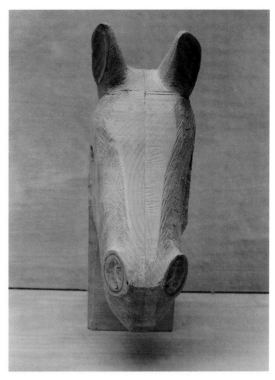

*Carved head ready for sanding.*

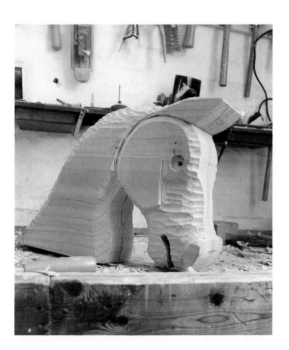

*Chiselling head, leaving cheek, nose and eye until last.*

(6) There is quite a sharp, straight dip between the front edge of the cheek bone and the slender bridge of the nose. This allows a real horse to see down its nose when its head is outstretched in full gallop, or when eating grass.

*Tip*
If you are carving with the head flat on the bench, leave the nostrils and part of the lower lip until last as this will help balance the head. When one side of the jaw has been completely carved, turn the head over to carve the other side and slide a piece of wood of the right thickness under the carved side. The carving of the jaw and mouth should be done very gently with a freshly sharpened chisel, or use round and curved surforms, as it is easy to knock the whole jaw off if the job is attacked too enthusiastically.

(7) Pull back the lips to reveal the teeth, with the mouth slightly open, as shown in the plans. This gives the mouth more life and allows the white teeth to shine out when the horse is painted, and a bridle bit to be inserted.

(8) Create a slope from the lower lip that goes under the jaw to the rounded chin.

(9) Using a fine-toothed tenon saw where possible, make a cut 5mm deep on each side at the base of where the teeth will be and chisel out the surplus to form the teeth.

## NOSE

The bridge of a horse's nose is quite narrow. It is broadest at eyebrow level, narrowing all the way down to end in a 'V' between the nostrils. At rest a horse's nostrils do not point directly forward or sideways, but somewhere between the two, which means that there are several different positions in which they can be carved. These include:

(a) with full round nostril standing out from the nose as if the horse is breathing hard. This is the position commonly found in the old rocking horse

(b) half open, as when trotting

(c) the resting position.

(1) Mark in pencil the desired angle of the nostrils, depending on which of the three positions is to be used: (a) is almost facing sideways; (b) halfway to the front; and (c) nearly pointing forward. Saw off the surplus wood with a tenon saw.

*Sawing off the nostril end in position (b).*

(2) On the two flat sawn surfaces left, draw the actual shape of each nostril and then carve out the nostrils to a depth of 5mm with a gouge to fit the inside curve. Using either a round surform or a round rifler file, take away the excess wood from the outside curves of the nostrils so that they stand away from the bridge of the nose and lips. A horse's top lip is very mobile so the edge of the nose should be about 22mm above and back from the edge of the top lip.

(3) After taking away the surplus wood with a chisel or gouge, most of the detailed carving of the mouth, chin and nose can be done with a round surform.

*Tip*

As it is difficult to sand the inside of the nostrils or ears completely smooth, put a little dab of wood filler in each nostril or ear and smooth it down with the finger tips, or leave them rough carved.

## EARS

(1) Draw in pencil the shape of the ears on the flat fronts. They should be as wide apart as the wood will allow. The widest part of the ear is halfway up, approximately 28mm, slimming down to the base, approximately 21mm, and tapering up to the tips, which on a real horse are quite pointed. For safety reasons, ears should be rounded on a rocking horse.

(2) Cut a 13mm slot between the ears with a tenon saw, taking away the waste wood with a flat 13mm chisel.

(3) Start to pare the wood from the front outside edges of the ears with a flat chisel and then do the same on the inside edges. Once the shape of the ear is established, finish the backs of the ears with a round surform, so that none of the back can be seen when looking square on to the ears from the front.

(4) With a 13mm gouge, scoop out some of the front of each ear to create a more lifelike effect. Do not make these hollows too deep or it will weaken the ear: 4mm at the bottom and getting shallower at the tip is enough.

(5) Tidy up between the ears with a small, flat rifler file and sanding paper.

(6) Using an electric hand drill, sand the face with a fine disc on a soft-backed sanding attachment. Finish sanding by hand ready for painting. It is very tempting to put the eyes in at this point, however if they are glass or plastic they are liable to be damaged while the rest of the work is being done. It is better to insert the eyes last, just before painting.

(7) When the features have been carved and sanded ready for painting, glue and clamp the neck overlays in position.

*Tip*

Freshly glued and clamped joints should not have their clamps removed until the time stated on the glue container has elapsed. Also, excess wood should be cut off wedges and dowels immediately after insertion, or when they are completely dry, as otherwise any slight movement may crystallize the glue and it will lose most of its sticking power.

(8) The back of the head and neck should be carved to slope over the overlays, outward and downward from the top of the neck in a long sweep to where the neck will meet the body. The neck is rounded at the front and back. Only sand the front of the neck and under the chin and throat ready for painting at this point. Sanding the head and body when they are glued together helps the neck to 'flow' better into the body, as there should be no sign of a join when the horse is completed and painted.

## MEDIUM BODY

The body of the horse is the easiest part to construct. It is literally no more than a thick-walled, modified oblong box with butt joints. Carving is required to make this oblong box into a curved shape, and for the detailed front area. There should be no angles as there are almost no straight lines on a horse, so there is quite a lot of wood to be chiselled and sanded away.

(1) Glue the two long and the two short pieces of wood together to make a hollow oblong measuring 66cm × 22cm × 23cm. This is the middle section of the body. When this is dry, plane any unevenness off the upper and lower surfaces. (This is where a planer thicknesser is extremely useful.)

(2) Saw out the leg sockets at each corner of the bottom plank, as indicated in the chart and diagram. This is for a plain butt joint.

(3) Put the top plank on top of the bottom plank (which is top side up), check that both are squared together, and clamp. On the top plank, mark a point 10cm from the front end and equidistant from each side. Do the same at the back end. Drill a 12mm hole vertically through both pieces of wood at the points marked. Unclamp the wood and put the hollow centre section between the other two.

(4) Cut two lengths of 10mm studding, the full thickness of the body less 2cm. Chisel out just enough wood around the holes in the top plank to allow the studding – with a washer and nut on the end – to be put through the holes to sit just below the outer surface of the top plank.

(5) Do the same on the outside bottom plank, but make the chiselled hole big enough for a spanner (preferably a box spanner) to be fitted to tighten the nut. There should be no metal showing above the surface of the wood. An alternative is to temporarily screw the top and bottom planks to the centre section, around the edge, and clamp the three sections together when they are finally glued.

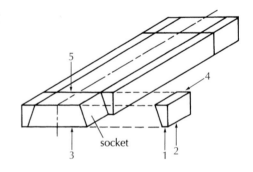

*Cutting out the leg and sockets.*

| TYPE OF HORSE | 1 | 2 | 3 | 4 | 5 |
|---|---|---|---|---|---|
| TINY CARVED | 20mm | 67mm | 64mm | 24mm | 54mm |
| MEDIUM | 41mm | 127mm | 114mm | 54mm | 95mm |
| LARGE ON SWINGER STAND | 41mm | 114mm | 140mm | 54mm | 121mm |

*Leg socket measurements.*

*Cutting out the rebate for the top of the leg in the bottom plank.*

*Tip*

If the top nuts start slipping when they are tightened, peen the studding over at the ends, which spoils a little of the screw thread and the nuts so that they cannot move.

(6) Draw a pencil line along the centre of the top plank, down the centre of the back, along the underneath of the bottom plank where the belly will be, and up the centre of the front – the breast – to meet the line on the top plank. This will help to ensure a balanced horse by providing a constant check that both sides are being carved evenly.

(7) Mark the top plank, where the head will be, by drawing round its base.

*Tip*

It is much easier and less frustrating to do most of the work on the horse while it is in three separate sections: the head, the body and the legs. If the general shaping and some of the sanding is done while the horse is still in pieces, the legs and head will not get in the way while carving and sanding the body, and vice versa.

(8) Now the body is ready for carving. The rump is a very good place to begin; there is plenty of scope for shaping as the horse's rump has to look rounded from all angles.

(9) Leave the very bottom corners of the middle section uncarved until the legs have been glued in position and the leg overlays are in place. It is very easy to carve too much away at this point as it is not the bottom of the horse. Be careful not to carve away so much at the top of the rump that there is not enough wood left to secure the tail in a 32mm deep hole. An alternative is to glue another piece of wood on the inside back of the middle section to accommodate the deep hole.

*Body blocks ready for carving.*

*First carving of body.*

(10) At the front, the neck should end in a short 'V', and most horses have an inverted heart shape which goes from between the front legs to about halfway up the breast. This heart shape is not essential, but it does provide an opportunity for some interesting carving (*see* photo on page 54).

(11) In the saddle area, from the points of croup the horse's back slopes by 13mm (or 25mm on the large horse) towards the bottom of the neck (withers). From the centre of the saddle area, the sides of the body slope downward and outward to halfway down the ribs, and then slope round and inward ending underneath to form a lovely rounded belly.

*Tip*
If overlays are to be glued at the top of the inside legs, then the carving on the body between the legs should not be com-

pleted until the position of the finished (carved and sanded) overlays fitted to the legs are marked on the bottom plank of the body. This will enable the body and legs to flow into one another without any gaps.

(12) Underneath the body of the horse, in the centre and 8cm from the back, there is a deep slope up to the back legs. This becomes a groove as it goes further between the back legs, then widens and deepens until it meets the furthest point at which the back legs or their overlays will be. The groove then goes up the centre of the back of the body and starts to narrow and become shallower until it finishes just below the point where the tail will be, halfway up the rump.

(13) You will notice that the sides of the neck flow straight into the body. There is no shoulder ridge at the side of the neck,

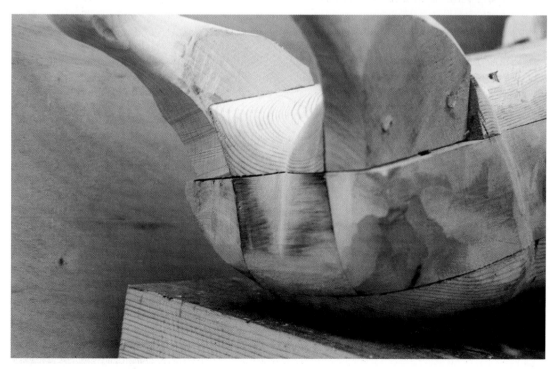

*Top of the legs and rump (pine).*

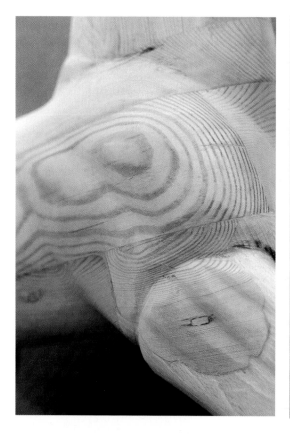

*Detail of front body muscles and top of the leg.*

*A little more shaping is needed.*

just strong muscles covering a bone that slopes from the withers to a point above the front legs. At this point it becomes bunched at the top of the forelegs. The rear end of this muscle follows through, shaping the ribs as it curves inward.

(14) There is a similar curve inward from the muscles just above the back legs to the ribs. This dip goes up the side of the horse to the point of croup.

(15) There is a slight curve upward from the centre of the belly and over the chest, just before the start of the forelegs. About halfway along and between the forelegs there is a gradual slope upward to meet the bottom of the inverted heart shape with its centre groove.

In addition to the basic details of body carving already outlined, there is plenty of scope to add further details, such as muscles and sinews, if you have the time and the inclination (*see* Chapter 9).

## WOODEN BACKREST

Instead of an almost flat saddle area to the horse, a wooden backrest can be added.

(1) This is a flattened half-moon-shaped piece of softwood that is inserted 13mm to 18mm deep across the back of the horse and at the back of the saddle, just in front of the point of croup, leaning backward by about 10 degrees. The grain of the wood is

along the back rest rather than across the thickness.

(2) It is about 25mm thick, flush with the horse's hips each side, curves upward between 38mm and 63mm (depending on the size of the horse) to the centre of the back, and is glued and screwed with two 50 × No. 8 screws, which are removed when the glue is dry and replaced by two 9mm dowels.

(3) Across the top edge, the backrest is chamfered so that it is parallel with the ground. It should be painted the same colour as the horse.

## MEDIUM LEGS

The rocking horse literally stands or falls on its legs, or more accurately its leg joints. The legs not only set the gait of the horse, they provide support for the rider and it is through the horse's legs that all movement is transmitted. Therefore, while the head of the rocking horse receives all the attention, it is the legs that do all the work. Put another way, if the head demands the best of a woodcarver, then the legs are equally demanding of a woodworker.

*Tip*
A word of warning: of all the timber chosen to make your horse, take the greatest care in selecting the timber for the legs. Strong hardwood with a good, straight, long grain and no blemishes is best.

(1) Cut out the shape with a bandsaw or its equivalent. The legs must be cut along the straight grain of the wood, as indicated on the plans, to give them the greatest strength.

(2) As an extra, 6mm thick pads, the same shape as the hooves and made of softwood, can be glued on to the sides of the hooves to give them a more rounded, authentic look. If the horse is going to be

on bow rockers, the rockers should be made after the legs have been glued to the body; if the horse is going to be on a swinger stand, the hoof rails are made first so that the legs can be fitted to them.

(3) Make sure the top 10cm of each of the four legs is completely flat, inside and out. Draw a line 6mm down from, and parallel to, the outside top of each leg. Form a triangle by marking the side of each leg with a line from the top inside corner to the pencil line. Cut off the triangular piece of wood across the top of the leg, leaving a slant so that each leg will fit snugly into the sockets made in each corner of the bottom plank (*see* diagram overleaf).

(4) In the top 50mm of all four legs, make three holes for No. 8 screws and screw the legs into place on the bottom plank of the body using 50mm screws. Check that the horse is standing correctly. Any adjustments can now be made to the legs by shortening the toes, or by paring small amounts off the sockets or tops of the legs.

*Checking a snug fit for the legs.*

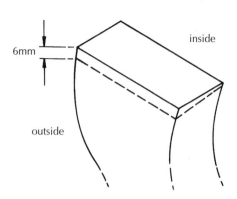

*Front leg.*

The maximum wobble that can be adjusted later when the rebates are cut in the hooves is about 9mm. A spirit level across the back of the horse will help to ensure a perfect upright position.

(5) The hoof rails should be made at this point if the horse is to have a swinger stand (*see* Chapter 5). Stand the horse on the completed hoof rails to make sure the hooves fit on the rails and that enough of the hoof overlaps the outside edge so as not to weaken the hoof when the rebate is cut out. Ideally, only half the hoof should be over the hoof rail. Adjust the leg joint if necessary. Check also that the swinger bars will have plenty of clearance each side when brought up between the legs.

(6) There is a further optional addition that can be made while the legs are still screwed to the horse – that is to put 13mm thick overlays on the top inside of all four legs where they meet the body, which reach down to the same level as the overlays that will be on the outside. Cut them from odd pieces of wood and chamfer the top edges so that they meet the body at the correct angle. As soon as they are glued and clamped into position, unscrew the legs from the horse and allow to dry.

*Underside finished with bolt holes plugged.*

### Carving the Legs

Like the head and body, the amount of detail that is put into the carving is the maker's own choice, so only a general indication is given here as to where details can be included. Leave the top 10cm of the outside of the leg free from carving.

The knee and hock joints are very knobbly and fatter than the leg, both just above and below the joints. The hock has a depression each side of the point of the hock bone. The knee is rounder but lumpier.

*The start of carving the legs.*

The lower leg is straight, but swells out to the fetlock, then narrows quite dramatically to form the pastern above the hoof, a point at which the straight grain of the wood is necessary.

(1) The rest of the leg should be carved as round as possible and the tendon groove that runs up each side of the leg from fetlock to knee or hock gouged out about 6mm deep, leaving the back tendon about 13mm wide. The sides of the hooves should also be rounded as much as possible, leaving the sole completely flat.

(2) If using overlays at the inside tops of the legs, fade away all the edges to nothing, except for the one that will be next to the body.

(3) Coarse and then fine sand the whole of the leg except for the parts that will be covered by the outside overlays.

(4) Mark the positions of the inside leg overlays on the bottom belly plank. Coarse and fine sand the rest of the belly ready for painting, then glue and screw the legs into position and immediately unbolt the rest of the body from the belly plank so that no extra glue can cause it to stick to the top of the legs.When the glue is dry, remove the screws, and drill and replace with 9mm dowels.

(5) If the horse is to be on rockers, they should be made at this stage (*see* Chapter 5).

(6) Stand the base (belly plank) with the legs attached on the hoof rails. If you are using rockers, the rest of the horse should be bolted or screwed together and the

head resting in place so the correct position of the rockers can be decided; this should be where the horse is balanced equally and not dipping at the front.

(7) Using a 25mm wide straight edge, lay it across the top of the hoof rail and flat against the sole of the back hoof, then draw a line across the hoof at the upper edge of the straight edge. Turn the straight edge upright and flat against the side of the hoof rail, with the edge against the sole of the hoof, and make an upright mark against the inside edge of the straight edge.

(8) Mark round the other two sides of the hoof in the same way, leaving the fourth side of the hoof unmarked. Put a cross in the marked off area so that there is no mistake when this part is sawn off to form the rebate to allow the leg to sit on the hoof rail. When all four hooves have been marked, turn the base upside down, with legs attached, and cut out all four rebates.

(9) Bolt or screw the horse together again and drop it on to the hoof rails or rockers to check that everything fits, and in the case of the hoof rails that the swinger bars can still move freely.

*Legs ready to cut out the hoof rebates.*

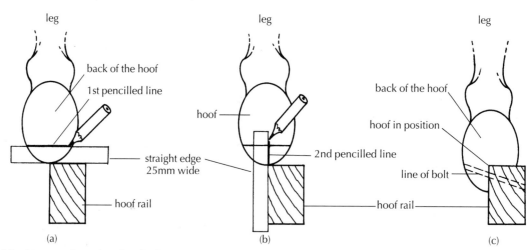

*Marking and cutting hoof rebates.*

(10) With a 6mm bit, drill through the overhanging parts of the hooves and through the wood of the hoof rail or rocker beyond. Slip a bolt into each hole as it is made so that the hooves do not move out of position. M6 roofing bolts are used, the actual length depending on the size of the hole that has been drilled. Partially countersink the heads of the bolts, leaving just enough proud so that they can be removed easily.

*Tip*

The hoof tips are now very vulnerable to chipping, so using the same hole, bolt an odd piece of wood larger than the rebate on to it to protect them while the rest of the horse is being finished. This is especially important with the large, heavy horses.

## BODY ASSEMBLY

(1) Now it is the turn of the head. Plane the bottom of the head and clamp upside down in a vice. Drill four screw holes to take 75mm No. 10 screws through the top plank, well spaced out within the area that will be covered by the head. Try the top plank upside down on top of the base head and neck, and screw into position. Drill pilot holes for the screws if necessary.

(2) Before final assembly, place the top plank (no head) on the middle hollow section, and then on to the bottom plank (with legs attached) to see if any unevenness has developed between the sections. Plane if necessary.

(3) With the head upside down in the vice, put the front bolt through the top plank. Smear glue only on the bottom of the head, then drop the top plank upside down on top of the head and screw tightly. These screws can be replaced by dowels when the join is dry.

(4) Spread glue on the upper and lower edges of the hollow middle, lower that into place on the top plank, then glue and place the bottom plank on to both of them. Thread the back bolt through the hole in the rump, put washers and nuts on both bolts and tighten. Leave to dry. (If the three sections are screwed together, it is better if they are also clamped to make the join tighter.)

(5) Draw a line 9mm from the top edge of the outside of one of the front leg overlays, and the same on the other leg. Saw off both top triangles of wood, as with the legs, to make a matching pair of overlays. Do the same with the back pair of leg overlays. This will quickly give the top edge the right slant so that each will fit exactly over the top of the legs and into what remains of the leg sockets.

(6) Glue and clamp all four overlays into position.

(7) Chisel the overlays into shape, tapering to nothing the further down the leg the shaping goes. The area at the top of each leg that was left untouched when the carving of the body was done can now be worked on to create the bunched muscles at the top of the front legs and the graceful curve that flows from body to leg at the top of the back legs.

(8) Coarse and then fine sand the neck and the body so that they flow into one another so that when the horse is painted there will be no visible join. Using wood filler at strategic points may help you, especially if this is your first horse.

(9) Before a final sand with the sandpaper on soft backing, carefully look the horse over for blemishes that need filling in with wood filler.

(10) Finally, sand by hand all over, not only to smooth the areas that cannot be done with a mechanical sander, but also to give you a second chance to discover any more holes that need wood filler, and to ensure that the surface is up to your standard of smoothness. Sunlight or a spotlight is needed for this; fluorescent light is

*Finished horse on rockers.*

*Body after first sand.*

not as good as it is too diffused. The use of an orbital sander for large areas cuts down on time and effort, but the last hand sand is very important. If the surface has been skimped it will show up when the horse is painted, especially on the face area.

## TAIL

It is better to drill the hole for the tail once the horse has been painted so there is no chance of anything dripping on to the sides of the hole and spoiling the strength of the glue.

(1) In the centre of the rump, about an eighth or quarter way down the back from the highest point, drill a hole 25mm in diameter and 35mm deep at an angle of about 20 degrees up from parallel to the floor.

## EYES

Finally, the eyes can be set in to give life to your horse. These are probably the most expressive parts of the horse, and it is a job that is comparatively easy to complete if ready-made plastic or, better still, glass eyes are used. Glass eyes give more of a glint than others.

The most important detail is the position of the eyes. Not only are they approximately a third of the way down the face, taking the line from the base of the back of the ears to the tip of the nose, they are also at either side of the head rather than the front. Remember: a horse in the wild must be able to look ahead to where it is galloping, and also behind to watch for predators. Its eyes therefore are not deep set but stand out from its head a little so that it has all-round vision.

There are two common ways of setting the eyes into the head.

*Position of tail hole.*

*Method One*

(1) Fill the eye sockets already drilled in the head with wood filler, and while this is still soft, push the eye into place with gentle thumb pressure. Any filler that oozes out should be smoothed away from the eye with the fingertips and later sanded to leave the eye round. When the horse has been painted, a black line, and maybe a red one as well, is painted round the eyes in an almond shape to give them an authentic slant. Traditionally, black eyelashes are painted above and below the black liner. If used, the red line should be just inside the black line. All rocking horses were painted in this fashion from the mid-nineteenth century onward.

*Type of eye detail from a G. & J. Lines horse.*

*Tip*
Use glass or plastic eyes with a wire embedded in the back as this can be cut short and curled into a loop which, when fitted, will embed itself in the wood filler and act as an extra precaution against the eye being prized out.

*Method Two*
(1) The second method is similar to the first, but the thumb pressure is exerted only on the bottom half of the eye when pushing it into the socket, giving the eye a realistic downward slant. The filler that has oozed around the edge is brought just over the rim of the eye, moulded to make eyelids and drawn to the sides in an almond shape, tapering to nothing in the corners. If not enough oozed out, some more may be needed to complete the eyelids and sur-

rounds. No painted liners or lashes are used with this type of finish; only a fine-bladed knife is used to carve the upper and lower lids into the soft filler. If the wood filler is very sticky, dip the blade into some water to stop the wood filler sticking to it.

*Tip*
If the horse is to be varnished, check the colour of the wood filler by wiping some on an odd piece of wood of the same sort as the horse, and putting on a coat of seal. If the wood filler is lighter, the discrepancy can be amended by adding a coat of coloured varnish (light oak added to clear varnish) very carefully, just over where the wood filler shows.

(2) The eye surrounds are now ready for sanding. Start with a No. 80 grit and

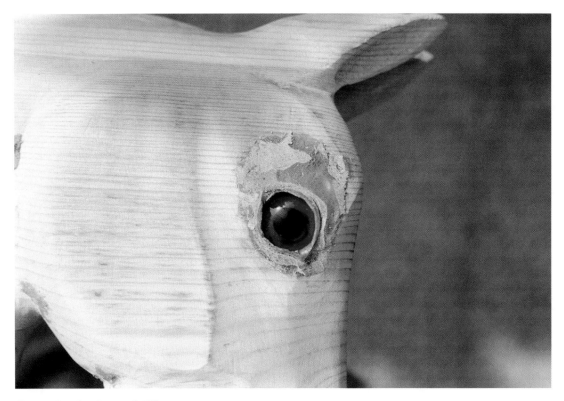

*Eye set in plastic wood filler.*

change to a finer one as necessary. Hand sanding is essential for these delicate areas as great control is needed to ensure the glass or plastic surface of the eye is not scratched, or too much filler removed.

*Tip*
When sanding near the eye, keep a fingernail between the sanding paper and the eyeball to protect it.

# ACCESSORIES

Except for mane and tail, without which the horse would look unfinished and bald, all accessories are optional and unnecessary if the horse is for display only. For a child's use, some accessories are needed, such as reins, saddle, stirrups, and stirrup straps. Details of all types of accessories can be found in Chapter 3.

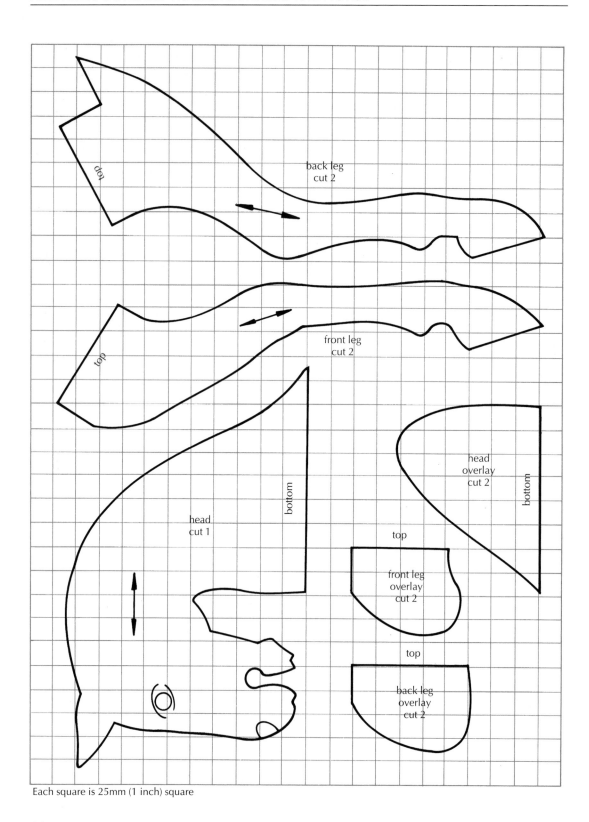

back leg
cut 2

top

front leg
cut 2

top

head
overlay
cut 2

bottom

bottom

head
cut 1

top

front leg
overlay
cut 2

top

back leg
overlay
cut 2

Each square is 25mm (1 inch) square

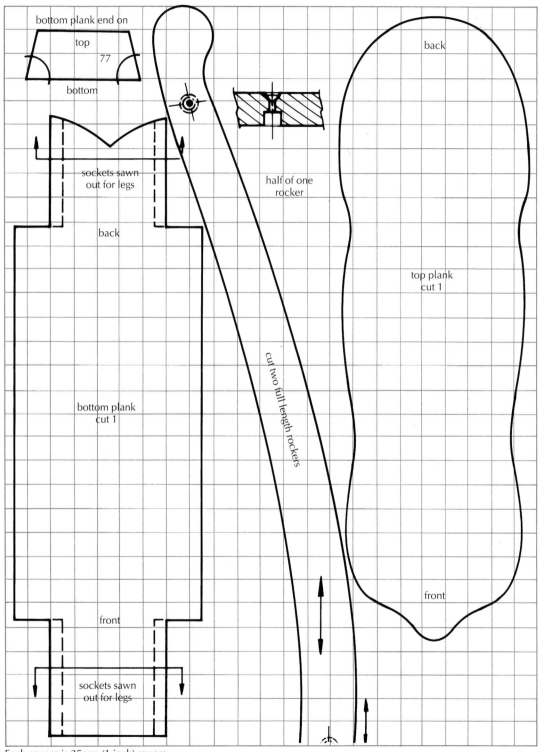

bottom plank end on

top

77

bottom

sockets sawn
out for legs

back

bottom plank
cut 1

front

sockets sawn
out for legs

half of one
rocker

cut two full length rockers

back

top plank
cut 1

front

Each square is 25mm (1 inch) square

# 5

# MEDIUM STANDARD HORSE: THE ROCKER OR SWINGER, AND FINISHES

The choice between a swinger stand and a rocker is generally a matter of personal preference; a child will be delighted with either. Those who favour a swinger stand, while admitting to some extra cost and time involved in the construction of the stand, will point out the extra strength and stability of the swinger, and also the evenness of the ride, which is an important consideration if the horse is intended to be used constantly by large numbers of children, for example in schools or hospitals.

Those who prefer the rocker will almost certainly do so because of its elegant and period style. It gives exactly the same sense of movement as that of a real horse at full gallop.

In addition, apart from being less awkward to move around the house, if well built and properly looked after, the lifetime of a rocker is at least equal to, if not better than, that of a swinger stand.

There are disadvantages to both rockers and swinger stands. Rockers are known as toe crunchers, and swingers as shin bashers. When rockers come to the end of their rock, they tend to slide along the floor (either backward or forward). Stands are supposed to stand still, which they do until the mechanism of the stand becomes worn, and then a larger child can grip the horse between their knees and hump it along the floor making a very satisfying racket! Swinger stands do not slide, but because they have moving parts they do wear and become loose over a number of years so they need occasional maintenance. Rockers have no moving parts so little maintenance is required unless the end spacers break away, as children are apt to stand on them to get an extra ride.

## ROCKERS

## MATERIALS

- Rockers: 2 × 32mm thick pieces of hardwood
- Spacer bars: 3 × 330mm long (approximately) pieces of hardwood, 22mm in diameter
- Platform: 5 × 406mm × 76mm × 15mm (minimum) softwood planks
- 26 × 38mm × No. 8 screws

*Tip*
The legs and rockers can be cut from the same piece of hardwood (1830mm × 360mm × 32 mm), as can the legs and hoof rails for the stand (1830mm × 320mm × 32mm).

## CONSTRUCTION

The rockers must be of a straight, long grain hardwood as they take the full weight of rider and horse, and the underside of each rocker is in constant contact with the floor so it gets plenty of wear. Boards and spacer bars can be constructed from either the same hardwood or a softer wood, depending on the style chosen. The rockers shown in the plans are for a medium horse and of the simplest style, but they can be adapted to many variations, including ornate shaping of the tops of the rockers.

There are several essential points in the rocker design which must be adhered to. Firstly, the lower edge of the rockers which are in contact with the floor should not have too steep a curve. Secondly, there should be a flattened area about 15cm along the centre of the bottom of each rocker, and thirdly, the grain of the wood must go correctly along the length of each rocker. The medium rockers are

the maximum length that can be cut in one length; any longer and the rocker must be cut in two pieces or the grain of the wood at the ends of the bow becomes too short which makes it weak enough to crack. The longest grain is always in the centre of the rocker, or for the longer rockers in the centre of each of the halves.

The rockers should always be braced in the centre and at either end to give a finished look to the cradle, stopping any tendency for the rockers to gradually spread out sideways with use, which would crack the tops of the legs of the horse.

(1) The plans only show half of the rocker, so a template should be made of the whole of the rocker before cutting the wood.

*Rockers can be altered to your own design.*

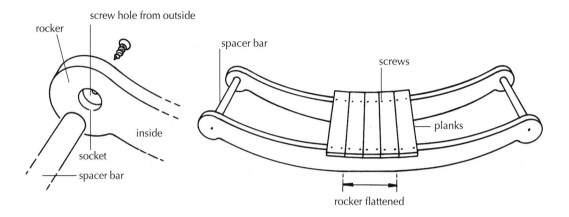

*End of rocker.*          *Completed rocker.*

(2) Cut out two rockers, and plane and sand the flat sides if needed, then clamp them together to smooth the inside and outside curves. It is important that the outside curves (bottom of both rockers) are identical, with no dents or bumps, so that they will give a smooth ride. The centre of this curve should also be slightly flattened for 15cm to prevent the horse from rocking when the rider is still mounting.

(3) While still clamped together, drill 5mm screw holes through both rockers, in the three positions indicated on the plans.

(4) Countersink the holes on the outside of the rockers.

(5) Mark the rockers so that there is no danger of turning one round and getting a mismatch. Then unclamp them, and on the inside flat surfaces of each, enlarge the screw holes with a 22mm spade drill to a depth of 8mm so that they will take the ends of the spacer bars.

(6) Measure between the inside edges of the toe tips of the horse (ignore the extra hoof pads if they have been added) and calculate the length of the spacer bar by calculating the distance between the toe tips minus 16mm. Do the same with the back legs. If there is a difference in measurement then the third central spacer bar measurement should be the mean of the other two measurements.

(7) The three spacer bars can be cut from dowel, or turned or carved in wood with 22mm ends to fit the enlarged holes in the rockers.

(8) Assemble the rockers using 38mm × No. 8 screws to check that everything squares up and that the hooves of the horse fit over the rockers by about half their width. When satisfied, glue and screw the rockers together. Immediately check that everything is square again and the three spacer bars are horizontal, then leave to dry undisturbed.

(9) Cover the screw heads with wood filler.

(10) Put the first of the five planks across the top of the rockers in the centre, and add the other four, two on each side. Check that they are all even then mark the ends where they overhang the rockers before drilling two holes each end to take 32mm × No. 8 screws. Countersink the holes and screw the planks in place. Chamfer and sand the edges and corners to leave nothing that is sharp or rough. Cover the screws with wood filler, then sand. The rockers are now ready to gauge the hoof rebates of the horse before they are painted or varnished.

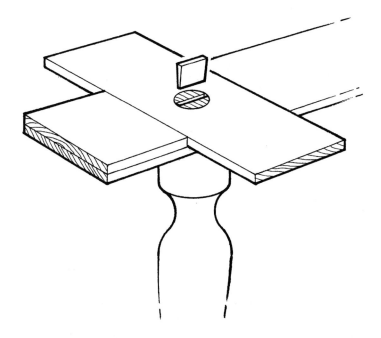

*Underneath one end of the swinger stand.*

# MEDIUM SWINGER STAND

## MATERIALS

- Top rail: 1 × 1300mm × 90mm × 32mm piece of softwood
- Bottom long plank: 1 × 1350mm × 120mm × 32mm piece of softwood
- Bottom cross plank: 2 × 430mm × 120mm × 32mm pieces of softwood
- End stop: 2 × 120mm × 75mm × 32mm pieces of softwood
- Pillar: 2 × 560mm × 90mm × 90mm (or 90mm diameter if turned) pieces of hardwood
- Hoof rail: 2 × 1230mm × 50mm × 25mm pieces of hardwood
- Wedge: 4 × pieces of hardwood, size as required and taken from off-cuts

- Clamps: 2 × pieces of metal to suit 10mm diameter swinger bar
- Swinger bar: 2 × metal rods, 10mm in diameter (*see* Diagram 20)
- Cap: 4 × pieces of metal to protect swinger bar ends.
- Base plates: 2 × pieces of metal or nylon to protect swinger bar and top rail from wear
- 12 × 38mm × No. 8 countersink screws
- 4 × 9mm gimp pins
- 12 × 9mm nails
- 4 × split pins (size depends on size of hole in the end of the swinger bar)
- 4 × 10mm thin washers

## CONSTRUCTION

The swinger stand was sometimes known as a safety stand because it superseded the old, very deep Georgian rockers, from which a vigorous rider could be thrown

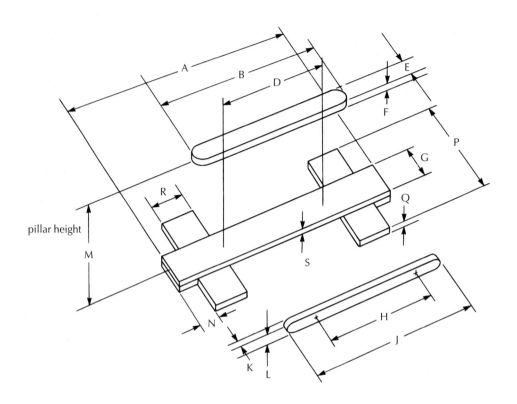

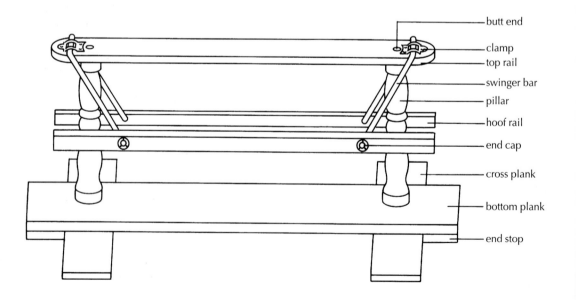

*The dimensions of a swinger stand and the fully constructed swinger stand.*

| Millimetres | A | B | D | E | F | G | H | J | K | L | M | P | Q | R |
|---|---|---|---|---|---|---|---|---|---|---|---|---|---|---|
| Large | 1,524 | 1,372 | 1,016 | 102 | 34 | 152 | 864 | 1,295 | 25 | 57 | 427 | 427 | 38 | 127 |
| Medium | 1,372 | 1,219 | 914 | 89 | 32 | 121 | 762 | 1,245 | 25 | 51 | 432 | 432 | 32 | 114 |
| Small | 1,118 | 1,016 | 813 | 76 | 32 | 108 | 610 | 1,016 | 32 | 51 | 356 | 406 | 25 | 102 |

*Measurements for swinger stands.*

over the head of the horse when it was at the end of its rock. It was also known as the American rocker as it first arrived from the USA. Details given here are for the medium-sized horse, but by using the diagram above and the chart on page 67, the sizes can be converted for either the small or large horse.

# BASE AND CROSS PLANKS

The base plank is at the bottom of the swinger stand frame. It is this plank that provides stability when coupled with the two cross planks. The cross planks must be positioned centrally under each pillar to give the pillars extra support. As important as the cross planks is the inclusion of a small stop underneath each end of the base plank, which prevents the frame being tipped up by a vigorous rider. These must be the same thickness as the cross planks.

*Pillars*
The two pillars can be carved, turned, or left square. They should be of well-seasoned, straight grain hardwood, and if turned, the 'land' at either end should be made slightly concave so that the pillars seat down on their circumference without rocking. Make sure the stubs are long enough to go right through the top rail, as well as through the base plank and cross plank at the other end. If the pillars are to

be square, take the first diameter measurement in the chart on page 68 as one side of the square pillar. The ends must be completely flat so that they sit properly against the top and base planks, and the 32mm square tenons should be quite straight and vertical, and long enough to go right through the top rail and base and cross planks (*see* the diagram opposite).

*Top Rail*
The top plank or rail holds the pillars upright and takes the whole weight of the horse and rider through the swinger bars.

*Hoof Rails*
The hoof rails keep the horse rigid and are best made of straight grain hardwood

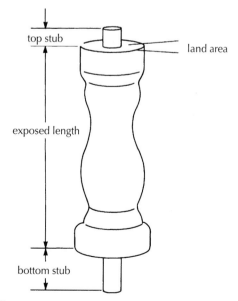

*Pillar.*

|  | DIAMETER | EXPOSED LENGTH | TOP SUB | | BOTTOM SUB | |
|---|---|---|---|---|---|---|
|  |  |  | DIAMETER | LENGTH | DIAMETER | LENGTH |
| SMALL | 75mm | 350mm | 25mm | 38mm | 25mm | 75mm |
| MEDIUM | 88mm | 400mm | 31mm | 38mm | 31mm | 75mm |
| LARGE | 100mm | 450mm | 38mm | 38mm | 38mm | 75mm |

*Measurements for pillars.*

without any blemishes. This is because most children use them as a natural step from which to mount the horse, they have to be very strong so that they can bear the weight of the rider in one small area. If softwood has to be used, the hoof rails should be at least 25mm more than the normal 50mm in depth, and the holes for the swinger bars sleeved with a nylon tube (metal can be used but it usually squeaks), otherwise the holes wear oval and the swinger bars rattle about, which causes more wear. It can also unnerve a timid rider.

(1) Using well-seasoned, good-quality softwood, cut out all the planks. Plane them if necessary and round the ends of the top rail and the hoof rails. Chamfer the top edges of all items (bevel them symmetrically), except the end stops.
(2) Glue, screw and countersink four 38mm × No. 8 screws underneath each of the two cross planks, that are at right angles to the top rail and above the base plank, central to where the pillars will be and equidistant from both ends.
(3) Measure and mark the centres of the pillars, 91.4cm apart on the top rail. Clamp the top rail on top of the base plank, central and equidistant from both ends. With a spade drill, drill two holes for the pillar stubs through the three planks. For square pillars, make two mortices 32mm square. The holes must be perfectly vertical which will ensure that the stubs of the pillars fit exactly. Unclamp the planks.

(4) With a tenon or bandsaw, cut a 'V'-shaped slot in the stubs or tenons of each end of the pillars. The slots in either end of the same pillar are cut at right angles to each other so that when the pillars are assembled the slots are at 90 degrees to the length of the grain of the top rail and the bottom cross plank, which will avoid splitting along the grain when the wedges are driven home.

*Drilling the hole in the stand for the pillar stubs.*

(5) The tapering slots are now ready to accept wedges, which should be made from the same hardwood as used for the pillars, and which are a slightly larger 'V' shape than the slots but the same width as the stub or tenon. The wedges are cut with the grain going down the 'V', not across.

(6) Using a tri-square, assemble all the pieces except the wedges, and check they are a good fit. Glue and screw each of the stops to the underside of each end of the bottom plank with two 38mm × No. 8 countersink screws.

(7) Glue the pillar stubs or tenons and assemble. Check that they are vertical with the tri-square and that the wedge slots are across the wood on the top rail. Smear the four wedges with glue, then drive them home firmly with a mallet. Wipe away any excess glue. If any stubs, tenons or wedges are left proud, cut off and sand immediately, then leave to dry.

## Base Plates

The base plates are essential to withstand the constant wear of the movement of the swinger bars. The best position for them is 76mm out from the centre line of the pillars, towards the ends of the top rail (90mm for a large horse). They can be made of sheet metal which is a minimum of 1mm thick and 6–9mm wide. It can be long enough to bend over the edges (in which case check there are no sharp edges) or just long enough to cover the width of the top rail and held in place with two gimp pins. Alternatively, they can be constructed from custom-made nylon (polypropylene),

76mm strips across, which do not squeak. A groove the depth of the base plate will need to be cut with a tenon saw and chisel into the top rail.

## Swinger Bars

The swinger bars are made from 10mm diameter iron, steel, chrome, or brass-plated rods. Solid brass rods are not advisable because the metal is softer and there is more likelihood of them being bent out of shape if the stand is accidentally knocked over or the horse is mounted continually from one side only. It is essential that the centre of the 'U' shape (E) of the swinger bars is exactly parallel with the two ends (I) that go through the holes in the hoof rails. If they are not parallel, the horse will not swing correctly and there will be wear on the top rail or hoof rail. The swinger bars and the holes in the hoof rail need to be placed correctly to get

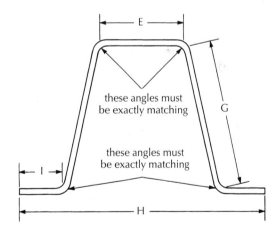

| | DIAMETER ROD | LENGTH G | TOP E | BOTTOM H | END I |
|---|---|---|---|---|---|
| SMALL | 10mm | 250mm | 75mm | 288mm | 44mm |
| MEDIUM | 10mm | 300mm | 89mm | 325mm | 44mm |
| LARGE | 13mm | 350mm | 100mm | 350mm | 44mm |

*Measurements for swinger bars.*

the best ride possible (*see* diagram and chart on page 69).

### Hoof Rails

(1) To save money, the two hoof rails can be cut from the same plank as the horse's legs (*see* the chart on page 69). Plane the sides, round and chamfer the ends, and sand away any sharp edges.

(2) Drill two 10mm diameter holes, 76cm apart and equidistant from the ends, through which to put the swinger bars. The holes can be sleeved (in which case the diameter must be increased to accommodate the sleeves) with either metal or nylon bushes, but it is not absolutely necessary as it takes years for wear to become a problem if good-quality hardwood is used. (Some woods may squeak without protection, however.) Shortening the measurement between the holes will bring the horse further above the stand, making it less stable. It will also buck and shy more steeply when rocked. If the holes are drilled so that the bars are vertical when the rocking horse is assembled, the horse will swing parallel to the ground with no bucking or shying at all, which is not so enjoyable for the rider.

(3) The easiest way to fix the swinger bars to the hoof rails is to first drill 2mm diameter holes, 2mm from the ends of each bar. Put the bar ends through the holes in the hoof rails and slip a washer on each one, then secure with a split pin through the holes in the ends of the bars. Cover these with a metal cap for safety. An alternative method is to put the washers on the ends of the swinger bars after they have been inserted through the holes in the hoof rails, then peen over the ends of the bars, rubbing off any sharp edges. With this method care must be taken that the swinger bars are not hammered out of true while the peening is done. It is also impossible to take the hoof rails apart once this has been done.

### Clamp

The swinger bars are held on the top rail by means of a bracket or clamp. As it takes a great deal of strain while the horse is in action, the clamp needs to be very strong and a good fit, therefore it is usually purpose-made of 3mm cast, or preferably pressed iron or brass with depressions across the middle that exactly fit the swinger bar. This is held on the top rail by M6 bolts or a combination of screws and bolts. Before final assembly, check the bar and clamp fit snugly without slop on the top rail, yet allow free movement of the bar. The stand is now ready for sanding and finishing.

# SANDING

This is a very dusty job, so it is advisable to do the sanding in the open air if your work areas has no dust extractors. The use of a dust mask is a must as wood dust can be the cause of chest infections.

The final sanding should be done by hand. Good light is essential in order to see the lines left by machine sanding. It is tedious, but is worth every minute of the time spent sanding by hand to get the small, difficult corners cleaned out and the large areas really smooth. Hurry this stage, however, and no matter how many coats of paint are applied, especially black, the blemishes will show through. If you are using gesso, the final sand should be done after the gesso has been applied.

### Tip

Now that the sanding is complete, if there is any doubt at all about the wood not being dry because it has been in a damp atmosphere, put the whole assembly somewhere it can dry out *slowly* for two weeks or more.

# FINISHES

There are three main methods of finishing a rocking horse: painting, varnishing or polishing.

Painting is the most popular with children as the horse can be made to look as close in colour as possible to a real horse. Painting is also very popular with first-time makers, as blemishes can be filled with wood filler, the colour of the wood or matching pieces is not important and the final effect is pleasing.

Varnish, especially clear varnish, can look very dramatic on a plywood laminated horse as it will show up every swirl of the wood. Clear varnish should also be used on a horse made from hardwood or carefully matched woods, as it will show up the colour and grain of the wood which it would be a shame to cover up. A sure

hand and good joinery are needed for this to be a success. A very hard, durable varnish such as polyurethane is ideal if the rocking horse is to have plenty of use and will be in constant contact with shoes.

Polish is not recommended for a horse that will receive a great deal of wear, or the owner will constantly be having to wipe off the fingermarks to keep the shine. It is usually only used on horses that are plain wood and intended purely for decoration. The preparation and polishing is an art in itself. There are many types of polish, as well as books on the subject, and I would suggest following the instructions on the polish container.

The finish always reflects the preparation underneath, which means that if anything has been skimped on, it will show. There can also be another one or two final stages, the traditional being a layer of

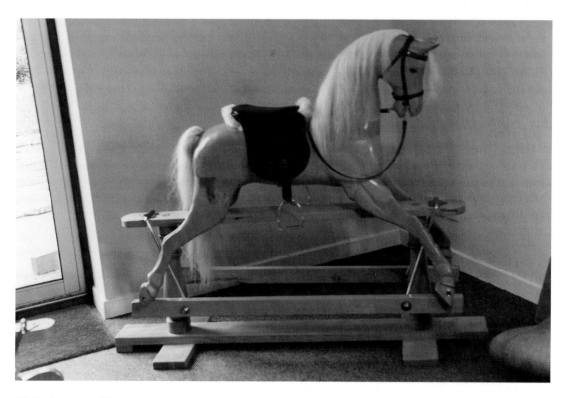

*Plain lime wood horse, clear varnished.*

gesso brushed on before painting; or sanding the wood well and sealing straight on to the bare wood, primer, undercoat and top coat.

Only paints and varnishes suitable for children's toys should be used. For both a painted or a varnished horse, the first coat applied is a sealer. When dry, this sealer raises the rough end grains and these can be sanded smooth. Then give the whole horse a light sand with grade 80 sandpaper, Garnet or similar. A second seal is now applied and the horse given another light sanding. These two seals soak into the wood and help to stop water absorption and therefore the movement of the wood.

For a painted horse, a layer of primer paint is applied after the seals, followed by a final check for blemishes that need wood filler. If blemishes do need covering, scrape the paint away at these points so that the wood filler will key in properly. Lightly sand the areas filled with very fine paper. Apply an undercoat of the appropriate colour, then paint with a top coat. Unless it is to be dappled, the horse can be finished at this stage with either a gloss or a matt clear varnish which gives a good, hard finish.

Horses that are to be clear varnished are painted with the first coat of varnish after the seals and sanded when dry. Further coats are painted or sprayed on, and the horse is lightly sanded in between with finer sandpaper each time until the desired effect is achieved. This can be up to as many coats as you wish. The last coat can be matt, satin or high gloss, the choice is yours.

### Tip
When painting the horse, rear it up and lean it against a solid support to paint the underside, inside the legs and under its chin and mouth. Then stand the horse on its hooves to complete the rest. In this way it is possible to apply the whole coat with the minimum of handling.

## DAPPLING

Traditionally, the rocking horse and rockers were painted. The horse was almost always painted a blue-grey with patches of dapple and finished with an overall clear varnish that went yellow with age. The rocker or swinger stand was either painted dark green or left as plain, clear varnished wood. Now, however, the more common practice, and certainly an attractive one, is for the horse to be painted white, with much more dappling applied, and the rockers or stand a natural wood protected with clear varnish.

Dappling is a black and white paint effect and there are a number of ways of doing it, depending on equipment, density of dappling required and maker's choice. Some practice is needed if dappling has never been attempted before. Any spray that is used must be compatible with the top coat of paint, for example enamel paint needs enamel spray. If this is not done, and an enamel paint is used for the top coat of the horse then cellulose paint sprayed on, when it dries the cellulose would begin to peel off. All types of dappling should be finished with a coat of varnish as the layer of spray paint is so thin that little shoes can soon leave scratch marks.

There are various methods of dappling.

### Method One
Finish the horse with coats of white gloss paint. When that is dry, using a small piece of soft sponge, dab small circles of black on to the body, letting the circles of black fade as the paint on the sponge is used up. Then start the process all over again. This fading gives a pleasing effect as a horse does not have the same depth of dappling all over.

*Method Two*

Use the same method as above but with a small stippling brush. This was the first method of dappling used on a rocking horse. It needs a lot of patience, as unless you are very practised it can take a considerable amount of time, but the effect is very good indeed, the dappling being either heavy or light as required.

*Method Three*

A quick and easy method, which is very effective on a small horse, is to stick little rounds of paper (price labels, for example) in strategic areas when the top white coat is dry. Then with a can of black spray of the same type as the paint, give a very light spray over the rounds of paper. When the spray is dry, remove the paper rounds. This works well if done only on the rump, neck, and muscle above the foreleg.

*Method Four*

After the white top coat is dry, spray the areas to be dappled very lightly with a can of black spray paint to give a mist effect. When this is dry, using a can of white spray paint, spray little spurts of white on top of the black. This resembles the real thing quite closely and is a reasonably cheap way of doing it if only one horse is to be made. However, it does require practice on an upright surface because if the white spray can is too close, the dots of white will contain too much paint and will drip. If the can is too far away, there will be only a mist of white rather than a distinct dot.

*Method Five*

(1) Using an airbrush, dilute the black paint (following the instructions that come with the airbrush) and spray small circles of black paint over all or part of the horse. This is closest to the dapple on a real horse as the variation of depth and size of the dappling can be so easily controlled.

Traditionally, dappled rocking horses had black ears and noses, black hooves and black on their hocks and knees, but this is not always the case with real horses. Finish the dappling with a clear coat of varnish.

## PAINTING TEETH

Only four teeth can be seen on each side of the horse's mouth, with the front two larger than the others. The gaps between the teeth should be as narrow as possible; wide gaps make the horse look as if it is snarling and is too fierce for some children.

The mouths of traditional horses were painted dark red, but in fact horses' mouths are much the same colour as humans' mouths.

These are the main finishes currently in use. No doubt there are others for individually designed rocking horses, that have the same pleasing effect.

The patterns for the Medium Standard Horse are on pages 60 and 61.

# 6

# SMALL PLYWOOD FILLY

It may be difficult to find suitable wood with which to make a rocking horse, so Chapters 6 and 7 include designs that rely almost entirely on plywood, which is easy to obtain from builders' merchants and DIY stores. Only use a good-quality exterior ply or it will be a labour of love that will not last long.

The Plywood Filly is a small horse made primarily from thick plywood, which makes it strong enough for small children. If care is taken with the finish, it can also

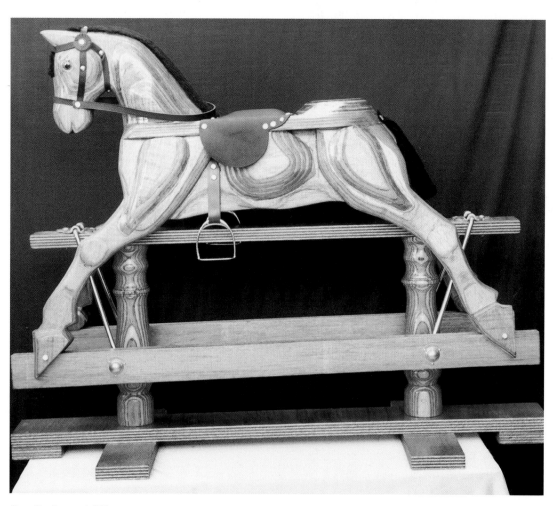

*Small plywood filly.*

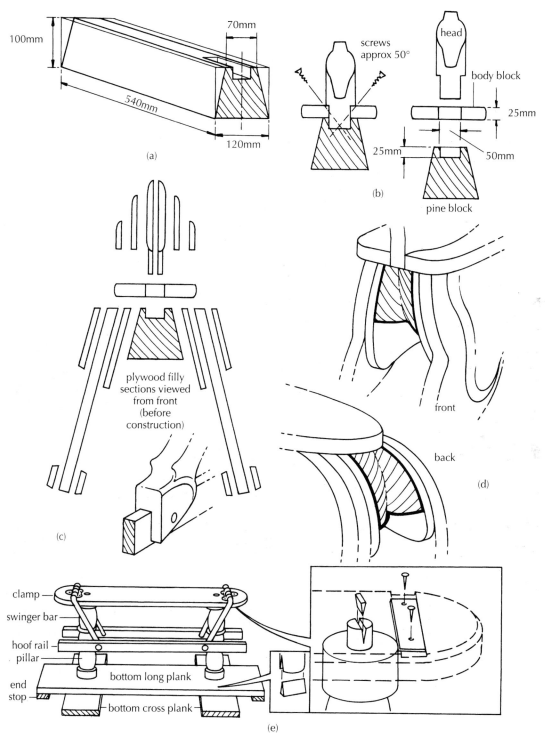

*Construction of the small plywood filly and its swinger stand.*

be a pleasing piece of furniture. It is not meant to be highly carved, just cut out, assembled by gluing, screwing and clamping, with one mortice and tenon to make, and sanded to show off the swirls of the different layers of coloured woods that make up the plywood.

**Dimensions:** 86cm high, 108cm long, 40.5cm wide and 66cm to the saddle.
**Time taken:** 25 hours minimum, plus time for drying and painting.

# TOOLS

- Vice or similar
- Bandsaw or electric jigsaw with fine blade
- Electric drill and stand
- Wood lathe (if pillars are turned)
- Power file
- Tenon saw and ripsaw
- 25–30mm chisel (if mortice is to be done by hand) or a morticer
- 2 × 20cm and 2 × 15cm (minimum sizes) G-clamps
- 1 × flat and 1 × round surform
- 12.5cm diameter rubber backing disc for drill sanding discs
- 2mm, 6mm, 13mm twist drill bits
- 22mm, 25mm spade drill bits
- Screwdriver for No. 8 screws
- Pencil
- Ruler
- Tri-square

# MATERIALS

- 1 × sheet of 2400mm × 1200mm × 25mm good-quality plywood (not necessary to use marine ply)
- 1 × piece of 12mm thick plywood, minimum size, 10.2cm deep
- 1 × 540mm × 120mm × 100mm block of softwood
- 2 × 30mm long dowels, 9–10mm in diameter (if used)
- 1 × pair brown glass eyes, 20mm in diameter
- Wood filler to match colour of wood or lighter
- 14 × 50mm × No. 8 screws
- 12 × 38mm × No. 8 screws
- 4 × 75mm × No. 8 screws
- Wood glue
- Wood sealer
- Polyurethane varnish

## MARKING & CUTTING OUT

(1) Start with the 540mm × 120mm × 100mm block of softwood (*see* fig. a). Plane the top and bottom of the body block, not the sides.
(2) Mark round and cut out all the parts of the horse from the sheet of 25mm thick plywood, except for the two body sides,

*Sanded head showing colours of the plywood.*

four neck pads, two face pads, four leg pads and eight hoof pads which are cut from the sheet of 12mm ply.

(3) Glue together the two head pieces, and when dry add the two face pads. Remove surplus wood to make the tenon at the bottom of the head only 2.5cm thick by sanding off the layers of ply.

(4) Cut a 12mm gap between the ears and tidy the edges.

(5) The tenon at the bottom of the head is 10cm long × 5cm high × 5cm thick. Reduce the thickness by cutting 7.5mm off each side to leave a thickness of 2.5cm.

(6) Drill a 6mm guide hole for the eyes straight through the head. Using the guide hole as the centre, drill a 22mm hole 15mm deep with a spade drill bit for the eyes at each side of the head.

(7) Chamfer and sand the face and ears (not the neck), and score out a shallow mouth with a tenon saw.

(8) Draw a central line down the top of the block of wood that is the body, down the centre of the back along the underneath (the belly) and up the front. Draw the same line along the back piece.

(9) Mark out two parallel lines 35mm either side of the line on the top of the body block, and on the front and back ends. Join these two lines with two lines marked 51mm out from the bottom centre line. Using a ripsaw, cut off the excess of wood so formed, then plane both sides. Check that the dimensions correspond to fig. 1a of the plans.

(10) Mark and make a 25mm square mortice in both the front top of the body block and also the front top of the back, to correspond exactly to the tenon on the bottom of the head. This can be done with a morticer or by hand using a saw, mallet and chisel. The criteria is that the mortice (or channel) has straight sides no deeper

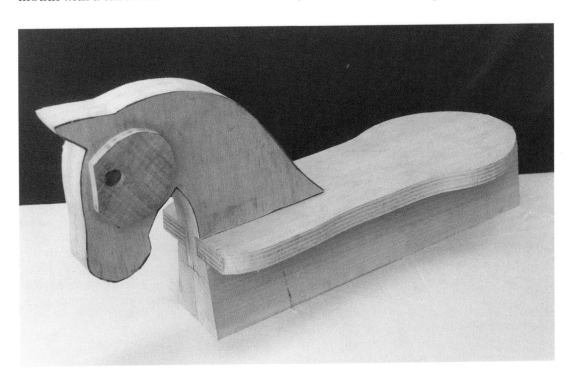

*Checking the tenon fits the mortice correctly.*

*The back with the mortice cut out.*

than the tenon and is only just big enough to slide the tenon into.

(11) Make a mark 12mm up from the bottom front centre of the body block to be used later for chest shaping. Draw a line either side of this centre mark going down to approximately 2mm in from the outside bottom corners. Then draw two lines underneath, gradually coming closer until they meet the centre line approximately 30mm underneath. Do the same at the bottom back, marking 25mm up the back and 40mm underneath. It is safer to do the actual shaping at stage (18).

(12) When dry, glue the hoof pads to the legs. Screw the belly sides and the four legs into position, as marked on the plans. Offer up the small belly pads and glue into position. When the two pads are dry, plane across the top of the two body sides.

Everything should now be level with top of the body block.

(13) At this stage make the hoof rails and insert the swinger bars so that the body with the legs attached can be set on the hoof rails to check that they are correct – that the hooves are halfway on to the hoof rails, with the other half over the outside of the rails.

(14) Dismantle the four legs and large belly side with small pads glued in position, and chamfer the legs to show up the grain in the wood and to take off the rough edges. Leave the bottom of the hooves flat. Also chamfer the small belly pads but not the top.

## ASSEMBLY

(1) Matching the parts of the mortice, glue and screw the large body back onto

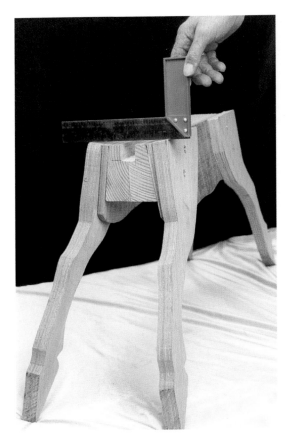

*Showing the amount of wood to be taken off the legs to make the top flat.*

the body block. Screw positions are marked on the plans.

(2) Glue and clamp the small rump pad in position.

(3) Glue and screw the tenon of the head into the mortice, checking that there is no gap between the base of the neck and the back. The angles of the screws are marked on the diagram on page 75. (The screws can be replaced with dowels if preferred once the glue is dry.) When finished, all screws must be below, and dowels level with, the surface of the surrounding wood.

(4) Glue and screw on the two large belly sides with small belly pads already in position. At this stage use surform to create the lower chest and rear shaping (as marked out in stage (11)). This is easiest if the horse is turned upside down; the groove is 11mm at the front bottom edge and 25mm at the back bottom edge). Fine sand the grooves and underbelly in preparation for sealing and varnishing.

(5) Glue and screw the four legs in position. Glue and clamp the four neck pads in position, making sure they are flush with the back. Glue and clamp the four leg pads in position.

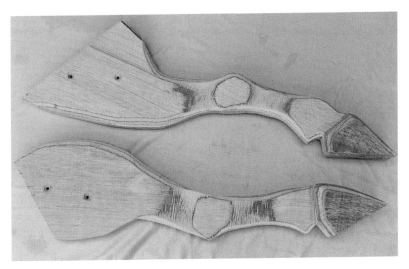

*Sanding and drilling the legs.*

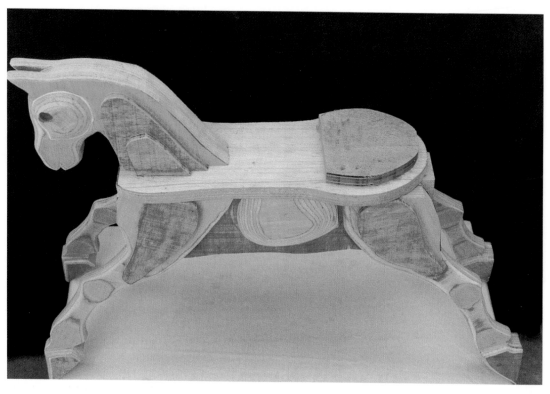

*Top glued on and ready for sanding.*

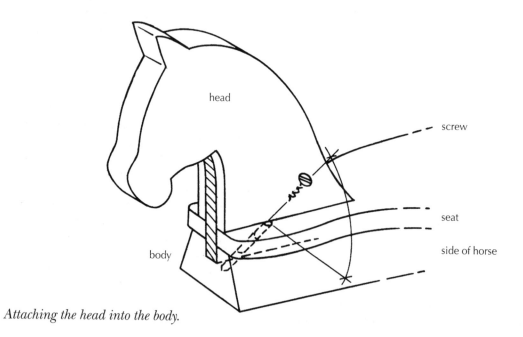

*Attaching the head into the body.*

*Pencil mark of the groove going up the rump.*

(6) Set the horse on to the hoof rails again and cut out the rebates in the hooves (*see* page 54). With a 25mm wide straight edge, draw a vertical line up the side of the hoof parallel to the side of the hoof rail both back and front, and 25mm up and horizontal to the hoof rail, across the hoof at the back side and front. Do the same with the other three hooves. Take the horse off the hoof rails, turn it upside down and cut out the rebates as marked.

(7) Sand the neck and neck pads so there is an even slope from the top of the neck over the pads to the seat and out towards front and back, showing up all the coloured layers of the plywood. Care should be taken with sanding so that no sanding marks are left on the wrong pieces of the horse, for example vertical sections meeting horizontal sections. (This only applies if the horse is to be plain wood.)

(8) Do the same with the back and rump pad, blending the front and back with the legs.

(9) Give the horse a general fine sand.

(10) Fill the eye holes with wood filler, and while soft gently press the eye in until it is nearly level with the wood surround. Wipe away any excess filler.

(11) Check the horse for any gaps in the structure, and fill with filler then sand by hand.

(12) Apply a clear sealer. When dry, this sealer will have raised the grain at the ends of the plywood, and this will need sanding down either by hand or very lightly with an electric sander of your choice. This process may need doing two or three times, but is worth it because it gives a much more finished look to the horse, and is more comfortable for the rider.

*Tip*
Try to find a wood filler to match the wood, however if the wood filler is paler than the surrounding wood, use a light or medium oak varnish and a fine brush to carefully cover the wood filler. This is only necessary if the horse is to be clear varnished.

(13) Stand the horse on the hoof rails again and from the outside drill a hole through each hoof and the rail to take a 60mm M6 Hex brass bolt.

81

*Sanding completed. Eye set in.*

# PLYWOOD STAND

Sections to be cut from 25mm plywood:

- Hoof rails: $2 \times 1000mm \times 60mm$
- Top rail: $1 \times 1020mm \times 75mm$
- Bottom plank: $1 \times 1020mm \times 108mm$
- Cross planks: $2 \times 406mm \times 108mm$
- $2 \times$ pillars:

(a) if turned on a lathe, finished size: diameter 75mm, exposed length 305mm; top stub diameter 25mm, length 38mm; bottom stub diameter 25mm, length 75mm.

(b) for square pillars, read square instead of diameter.

- $16 \times 38mm \times$ No. 8 screws (plus wedges as required)

The base plank is the plank at the bottom of the swinger stand frame. The cross planks are the other two planks at the bottom of the frame and are set at right angles to the base plank and centrally under the pillars to give them extra support. Under each end of the base plank is a stop of exactly the same thickness as the cross planks, which prevents the stand from being tipped up by a vigorous rider. See Chapter 5 for further details.

## PILLARS

The two pillars can be turned or left square. If turned, start with a 75mm plywood square – four pieces of 25mm good-quality ply glued together. Do not do any fine shaping as it is inclined to crumble, so leave the shaping simple.

82

The 'land' on either end should be slightly concave so that the pillars seat down on their circumference without any rocking. The stubs must be long enough to go through the top rail and through the base plank and cross plank at the bottom.

If the pillars are to be 75mm × 75mm square, the ends must be completely flat so they sit properly against the top and bottom planks and so the 32mm square tenons are quite central and vertical. They must also be long enough to go through the top rail and the base plank and cross plank. The top rail holds the pillars up straight by gluing the landing and the stubs in the mortice holes. The hoof rail keeps the horse rigid. It has to be strong as most children use it as a step with which to mount the horse.

(1) Cut out all planks along the top grain of the plywood. Round the ends of the top rail and the hoof rails. Chamfer the top edges of all items except the end stops.

(2) Using four 38mm × No. 8 screws, glue and screw each of the two cross planks underneath and at right angles to the base plank, central to where the two pillars will be. Clamp the top rail along the centre of the top of the base plank and equidistant from both ends. Measure and mark the centres of the pillars 61.5cm apart on the top rail. With a 25mm spade bit, drill the two holes for the pillar stubs through all three planks; for square pillars, make two mortices 32mm square. The holes must be completely vertical so that the pillar stubs will fit perfectly. Unclamp the planks.

(3) Using a tenon saw, cut thin 'V'-shaped slots in the stubs or tenons at each end of the pillars. The slots in the same pillar are cut at right angles to each other so that when assembled the slots are at 90 degrees to each other across the grain of the surrounding wood. Make wedges from offcuts, just slightly bigger than the 'V'-shaped

slots, with the grain going down the 'V' rather than across.

(4) Using a tri-square, assemble all pieces except the wedges and check for a good fit. Adjust the size of holes or stubs if necessary.

(5) Using two 38mm × No. 8 screws, glue and screw the stop underneath each end of the base plank.

(6) Glue the 'landings' and pillar stubs or tenons and assemble. Check that the pillars are vertical and the 'V'-shaped slots are across the top rails. Smear the wedges with glue and drive home firmly with a mallet, wipe away any excess glue, cut off any excess wedge and sand down when dry.

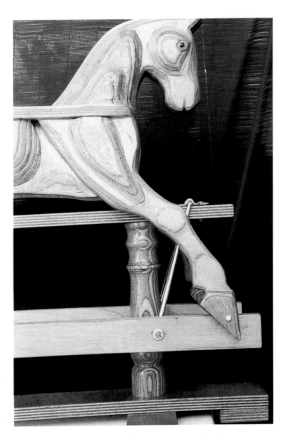

*Showing details of pillar and stand when completed. Protection cap still to go on the hoof rail.*

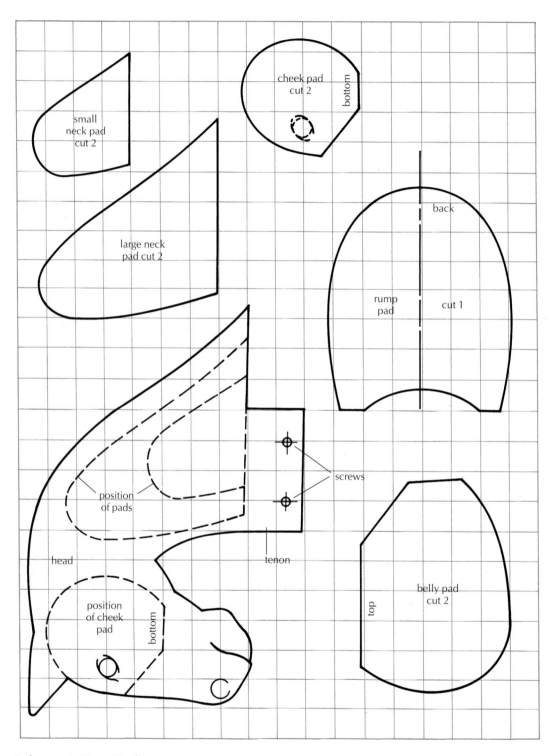

Each square is 25mm (1 inch) square

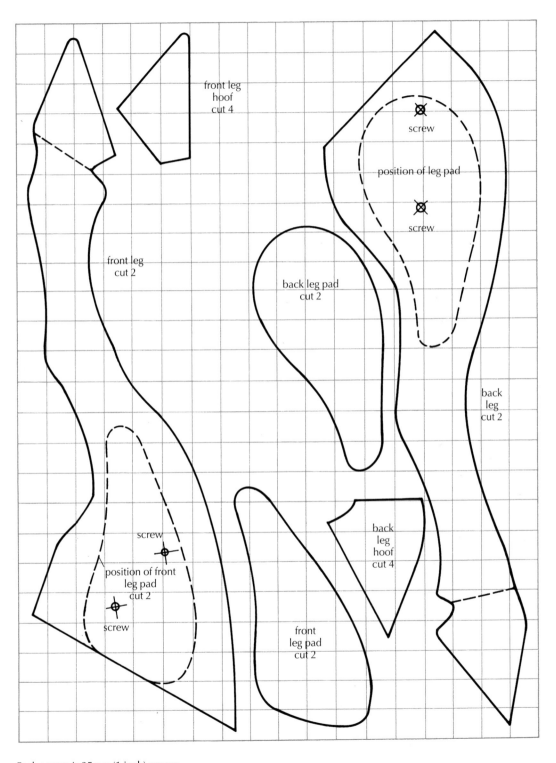

Each square is 25mm (1 inch) square

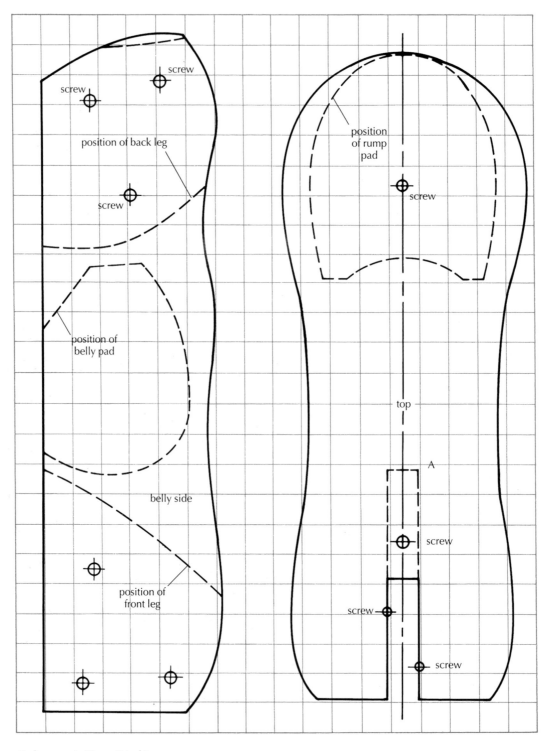

Each square is 25mm (1 inch) square

(7) In the sides of the hoof rails, drill two 13mm diameter holes, 76.2cm apart and equidistant from the ends, to take the swinger bars.

(8) Saw a slot 13mm wide × the depth of the base plate across the top rail, 10cm from the centre of the pillar and towards each end of the rail. Nail a base plate in each with two gimp pins (and/or glue).

(9) Slot the ends of the swinger bars and bushes into the holes in the hoof rails. On the other end, put a washer over the end of the swinger bar and hold in place with a split pin. Cover with a brass protection cap nail held in place with three 1.6 × 9mm brass pins. Hang the two swinger bars over the top rail and on the base plates, and hold fast with a clamp held in place with

an M6 × 40mm bolt and two 25mm × No. 8 brass screws.

# FINISH

Leave an unpainted strip up the forehead, over the head and down the neck for the mane and forelock, which are glued in after painting or varnishing.

Treat the stand with wood sealer in the same way as the horse, and sand down to get rid of the roughness. The horse and stand can be left as plain wood with a clear polyurethane varnish, coloured varnish or painted with an undercoat and then a top coat. Dappling can be effected by using a can of black spray paint (make sure it is

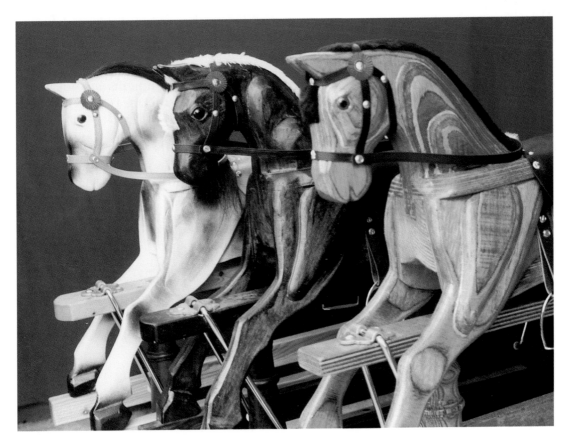

*Some choices in finishes.*

compatible with the existing paint) over a white top coat, and finishing with clear varnish to stop small shoes scratching the dappling.

# ACCESSORIES

## SWINGER STAND

- 2 × 10mm swinger bars plus split pins and washers
- 2 × nylon base plates plus pins
- 2 × 10mm brass clamps
- 4 × nylon bushes
- 4 × brass caps
- 12 × 5mm × 9mm brass pins (for fixing caps)
- 2 × M6 × 40mm brass coach bolts
- 4 × 25mm × No. 8 brass screws
- 4 × hex 60mm brass bolts (for fixing hooves to hoof rail)

## HORSE

- Fur fabric mane and tail
- Saddle
- Bridle and reins
- Brass-domed nails
- Daisy nails
- Brass or ribbon rosette
- Stirrups and stirrup straps
- Small rosette

A mane and tail can be made from fur fabric. Cut a strip of fabric (with the pile lying down the length of the fabric) 4.7cm long × 0.4cm wide, and another 2cm long × 1cm wide. After the horse has been varnished, glue the longer strip of fur fabric on to the neck and head of the horse where the wood has been left bare (make sure the fur lies flat down the neck); the bridle helps to hold it there.

Fold the second piece of fur fabric in half lengthways, with the fur on the inside and laying down the length of the tail. Sew across this bottom edge and up the side. Turn the tail right side out, with the fur laying down the tail. Nail a piece of 7cm × 1.2cm strapping across the top of the tail and the rump of the horse to neaten it.

The 25cm long stirrup straps are looped through the stirrups and the ends screwed to the side of the body between the front leg and the small body pad, with two 25mm × No. 8 brass screws and cups to match.

Further embellishments include a bridle of 1.2cm leather, a red rosette with 10mm brass-domed and daisy-topped nails, and a strong leather rein, 6.2cm long, screwed to the sides of the face just above the mouth with two 12mm screws with cups. A little saddle-shaped seat, again nailed with decorative nails, completes the horse.

This accessory set is designed for simplicity and to keep down costs. However, real horsehair manes and tails can be used, as for carved horses.

# 7

# PUSH-ME PULL-ME ROCKING HORSE

The plans are for a rocking horse that needs two children of roughly the same size to make it rock smoothly, and is ideal for use in a playschool or nursery. The children need to be old enough to make it rock to a rhythm or there will be chaos; an older child can manage on their own, but not with as much fun. Except for strengthening battens on the inside, the horse is made entirely of thick plywood.

**Dimensions:** Body length 810mm; height including stand 868mm; height to saddle 680mm; overall length including stand 1,340mm.
**Time taken:** 50–60 hours.

## TOOLS

- Protractor
- Marker/pencil
- Tri-square and straight edge
- Tenon saw
- Ripsaw
- Band saw or jigsaw
- Plane
- Round rasp
- Screwdriver to fit screws
- Pillar drill
- Portable drill
- Belt or disc sander with 40, 60, 100 grit
- Tape measure
- Glue
- Workmate or vice
- Mallet
- Chisel with flat, 25mm blade
- Bit for pilot holes, to take the screws
- Countersink bit
- 6mm bit for pilot holes for eyes and handles
- Clamps
- 22mm spade bit for eyes
- 13mm power file
- Spade bit for handles, size dependent on diameter

## MATERIALS

- 1 × 1350mm × 1350mm × 25mm good-quality piece of plywood
- 1 × 1000mm × 1000mm × 12mm good-quality piece of plywood.
- 2.5m of 45mm × 25mm softwood batten
- 500 × 25mm dowel for handles
- 2 × pairs of brown glass eyes, 20mm in diameter

*Tip*
When cut, mark each piece of ply as left or right, front or back, inside or outside, so there can be no confusion, as there are two heads and two pairs of front legs.

Sections to be cut from 25mm plywood:

- Top plank: 1 × 800mm × 170mm
- Bottom plank:1 × 800mm × 140mm
- Legs: 4 × 630mm × 580 mm (if cut from the same piece of plywood)
- Heads: 4 × 320 × 960 mm (if cut from the same piece of plywood)

*Most parts of the horse.*

- End sections: 2 × 130mm high, 130mm wide at the bottom, 70mm wide at the top. These must be measured accurately (*see* diagrams on page 92)
- Pieces: 2 × 180mm × 80mm.A & C
- Pieces: 2 × 180mm × 94mm.B & D

Sections to be cut from 12mm plywood:

- Body sides: 2 × 800mm × 190mm
- 2 × belly pads
- 8 × hoof pads
- 4 × cheek pads
- 4 × large neck pads
- 4 × small neck pads
- 4 × leg pads
- 8 × 25mm × No. 6 screws
- 34 × 50mm × No. 6 screws
- 14 × 60mm × No. 6 screws
- 4 × 32 mm × No. 6 screws

- 2.5m of 45mm × 25mm softwood batten, to be cut as instructions:
  2 × 746mm long pieces (check before cutting)
  2 × 386mm long pieces (check before cutting)
  Handles: 1 × 20–25mm in diameter and approximately 24cm long

## HEAD

(1) Glue the four sections to make the two heads. When dry, glue the face pads into position, as shown on the plans.
(2) Place each head in turn on the pillar drill stand, propped with an odd piece of 12mm ply or similar to keep the surface level. Drill one pilot hole for each of the pairs of eyes and also for each pair of handles, as indicated on the plans. Using a

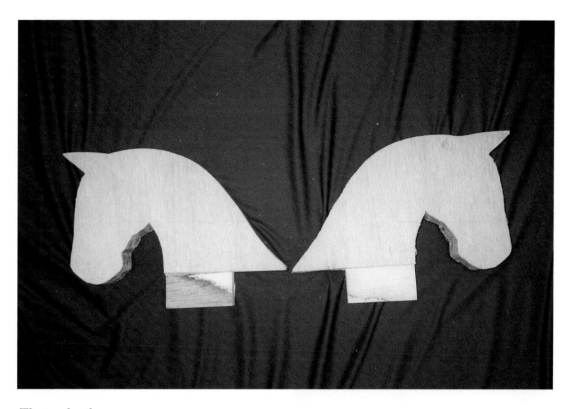

*The two heads.*

22mm spade drill, drill the eye sockets to a depth of 10mm. Drill a hole for the handle with a spade drill to suit the diameter, and this time drill right through the top of the neck. The holes must be a tight fit for the handle otherwise children will soon work them loose which will spoil the toy.

(3) Cut the tenon for each head by making the bottom of the head only 25mm wide. This requires you to take 12.5mm off each side of the 100mm × 50mm section attached to the rest of the head.

## BODY

(4) Mark a line along the middle of the 800mm × 170mm top, down the face, along the middle of the underside and up the other end to meet the top line. At each end and 12.5mm out from the centre line, draw lines parallel with the centre line, of 100mm each. Join the two ends to make an oblong that is 100mm long by 25mm wide.

Note: all the internal sections need to be angled on at least one edge.

(5) Draw along the middle, back and front of both end planks. Clamp them back to back, and at the smaller end (70mm wide) mark off a square which is 25mm wide × 25mm deep, being 12.5mm each side of the centre line. Cut out the square so formed to make part of the mortice for the head. Separate the two ends and temporarily screw them in place with 3 × 50mm × No. 6 screws under the ends of the top plank, centrally with a 50mm space each side.

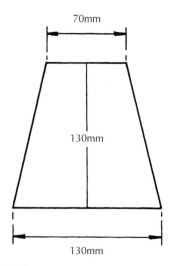

*End section of body.*

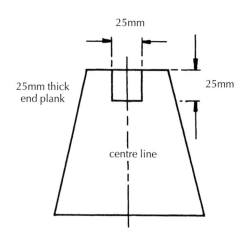

*End section of body with mortice cut.*

*Cutting out both ends of the mortice in the top plank and end sections.*

(6) Place the 180mm × 94mm × 25mm thick piece of plywood (marked B) on top of the 180mm × 80mm × 25mm thick piece (marked A). Make sure the ends are level and piece A is in the centre of piece B, and using 4 × 32mm × No. 6 screws, screw through piece B.

(7) 5mm in from the top corner of the smaller piece of ply A, draw a line at 102.5 degrees towards the corner of the larger piece of ply B. Do the same with the other three corners. Saw off the long triangles so formed.

(8) Do the same to the other two pieces of wood marked C and D. Unscrew the wood marking which two pieces of wood go together.

(9) Turn the top plank over. Glue and screw the smaller side of the piece of plywood marked A (using the same four screws and holes as used before) to the end of the underneath of the top plank. It should be placed centrally along the underside and butted to the end of the plank. Do the same with C at the other end.

(10) When dry, cut out the mortice marked out on the top side of the top plank, cutting right through the small piece of plywood A (or C) that is now

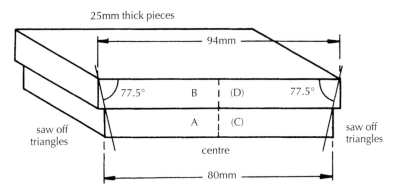

*Two inner pieces.*

glued underneath, and through the end plank which is still in position, making sure the tenon of both the heads are a tight fit when put in the mortice. Take the four 32mm screws out.

(11) Using four 60 mm screws and the same (countersunk) holes as before, glue and screw the large piece of ply B on to the smaller piece A and through into the top plank. Do the same with C and D at the other end.

(12) Measure and cut off two × 386mm long pieces of 45mm × 25mm softwood batten to put along each side underneath the top plank, between A and C, to give the body extra strength. Check them in place and then plane off 25mm from the

*Mortice, two inner pieces and battens.*

93

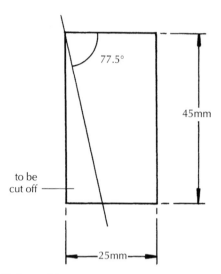

*Softwood batten.*

outside of each batten, leaving it angled at 77.5 degrees.

(13) Using two 60mm × No. 6 screws, glue and screw the battens carefully into position, placing them so that there will be a smooth angled edge right along and under the top to which to fit the two sides of the horse's body. Unscrew the end planks from the top plank.

(14) Plane a strip off each side of the bottom plank so that the angle is 77.5 degrees from the bottom edge. Using six 50mm × No. 6 screws, screw the end planks temporarily in place on top of each end of the bottom plank and carefully measure the distance between these two end planks, then cut two lengths of batten to fit, the same as for the top plank. Plane off the square 25mm outer edge of the batten to an angle of 77.5 degrees (*see* diagram on page 93). Using three 60mm × No. 6 screws, glue and screw each batten in place so that the sides of the horse can be attached perfectly. Unscrew the end planks.

(15) Glue and screw the two heads in position, making sure the bottom of the backs of the necks which are behind the tenons are glued to the top plank. From each

*Bottom plank and battens – a perfect match.*

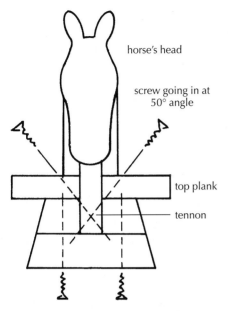

*The tenon of the head fitted into the mortice, showing the angles for the four fixing screws.*

(16) Glue and screw each end plank back into place so that they are also glued to the inside pieces A and B or C and D, and to the softwood batten at the bottom. Leave to dry. All screws on the outside of the body should be flush or below the surface of the wood.

(17) After planing an angle at the top of both sides of the horse so that they fit properly under the top plank, as in the photo on page 79, glue and screw them into position using the screw holes indicated on the plans: eight 25mm × No. 6 screws under where the belly pad will go, and eight 50mm × No. 6 screws near to the four corners on each side where the legs will be.

## LEGS

(18) Glue and clamp on the hoof pads.

(19) Offer up the legs in turn to mark, plane and check the angle at the top of each leg so that it fits flush under the top plank. At the same time, mark on the inside of the leg where the bottom edge of the side comes to so that the leg is not chamfered beyond this line.

side, screw a 60mm × M6 through the neck, into the tenon, and into piece A or C at a 50-degree angle. Then screw two 50mm × No. 6 screws underneath and into each of the tenons via planks B and D.

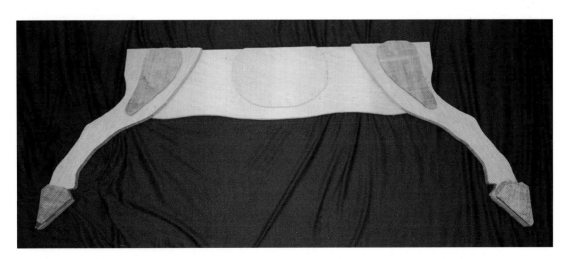

*The legs are offered up to see that everything fits together.*

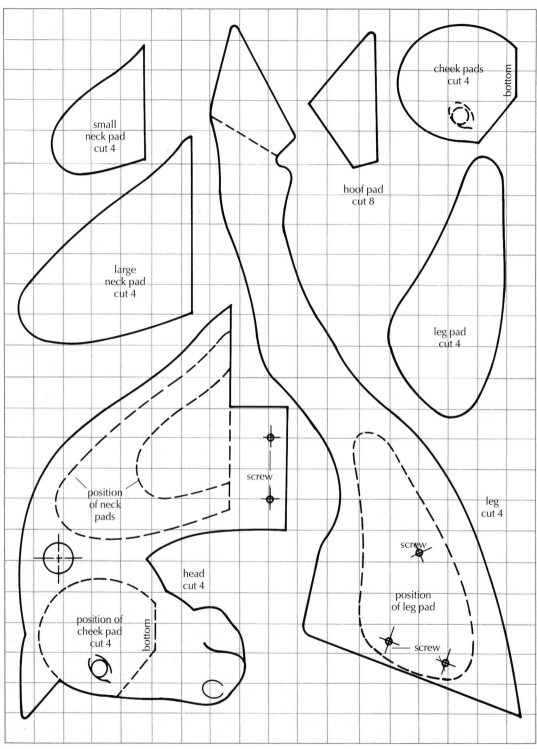

small
neck pad
cut 4

large
neck pad
cut 4

cheek pads
cut 4

bottom

hoof pad
cut 8

leg pad
cut 4

position
of neck
pads

screw

leg
cut 4

head
cut 4

screw

position
of leg pad

position of
cheek pad
cut 4

bottom

screw

Each square is 25mm (1 inch) square

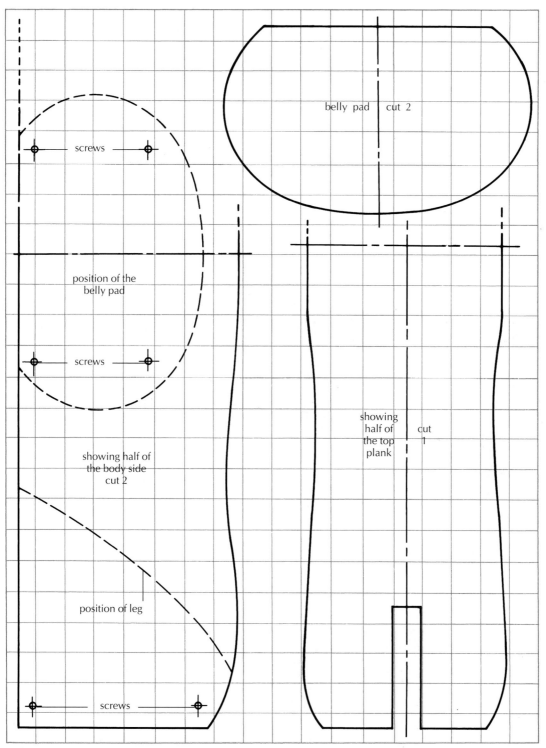

belly pad    cut 2

screws

position of the
belly pad

screws

showing
half of
the top
plank

cut
1

showing half of
the body side
cut 2

position of leg

screws

Each square is 25mm (1 inch) square

(20) Chamfer the legs, as outlined in Chapter 6. Smooth only the bottom of the hooves.

## ASSEMBLY

*Tip*

If you do not have big enough clamps to clamp the pads, use small screws instead. Remove the screws when dry and fill the holes with wood filler.

(21) Glue and screw the legs into position, as marked on the plans.
(22) Glue and clamp on the belly pads over the central position of the four screws in the side of the horse.

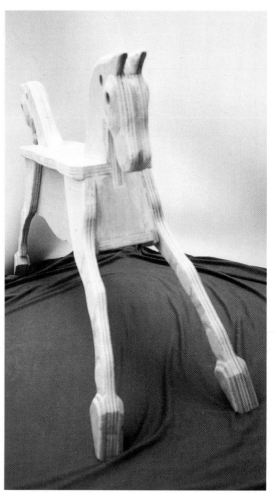

*Glue and clamp the leg and belly pads, and then it is ready for the first chamfer sand.*

*Glue and clamp the pads on.*

(23) Glue and clamp on the large neck pads, and when dry do the same with the small neck pads.
(24) Glue and clamp on the leg pads, as marked on the plans.
(25) The horse is now ready for chamfering. Take off the rough edges and smooth out all the ridges of the pads.
(26) Fit the eyes, as described in Chapter 4.
(27) Round off each end of the handles. Push them in, and when they are part way,

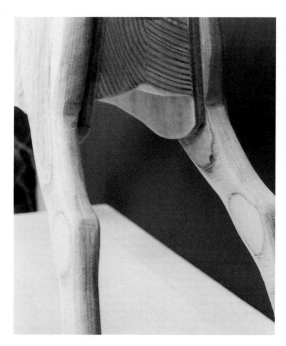

*The front of the horse after sanding.*

put glue on the middle and then push them further in so that the protruding area on each side is the same length.

(28) See Chapter 6 for instructions on how to set the horse on the hoof rails (without taking the legs on and off the body).

(29) When dry, paint the whole horse with a sealer. This will roughen up the edges of the plywood. Give it a good sanding all over and then paint on another sealer. When dry, give it a much gentler hand sand. Repeat until the whole horse is smooth.

(30) Now you can paint the horse as you wish using child-safe paints.

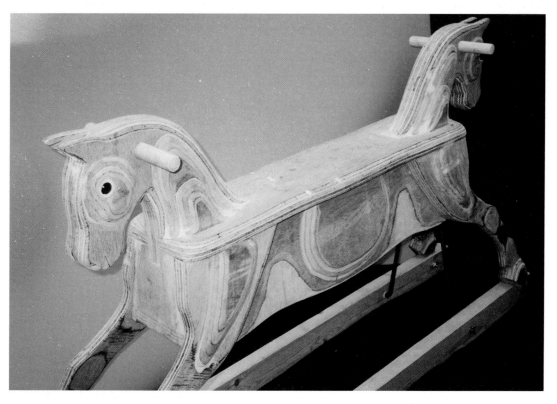

*Sanding done showing wood filler in places.*

*Hand dappling with a sponge.*

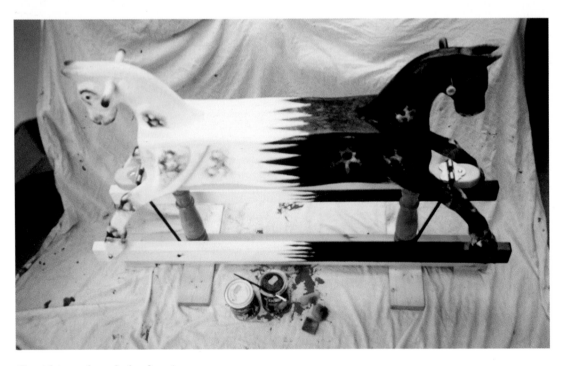

*Complete and ready for dressing.*

# STAND

Made from pine (softwood) with hardwood pillars and hoof rails (the hoof rails can also be in a thick softwood).

- Top rail: 1 × 1120mm × 75mm × 32mm (96cm between clamp centres)
- Bottom plank: 1 × 1180mm × 115mm × 25mm
- Cross planks: 2 × 410mm × 115mm × 25mm
- End stops: 2 × 115mm × 50mm × 25mm
- Pillars: 2 × 150mm plus ends 90mm in diameter (centre between pillars 73.5 cm)
- Hoof rails: 2 × 1350mm long, 32mm wide and 70mm high in good-quality softwood (75cm between centres of the holes for the swinger bars)

Follow the instructions given for the Standard Medium Horse (*see* Chapter 4) to make up the stand.

# ACCESSORIES

- 2 × horse hair or paint-on manes
- 1 × 43cm × 20.5cm saddle, plus nails for fixing
- 2 pairs of 7.3cm metal stirrups
- 4 lengths of 16mm strong leather strapping for stirrup straps, plus 8 × 25mm × No. 8 brass screws and cups to fit
- 2 × small clamps to take 1cm swinger bar
- 2 × iron rods either plated or painted, and 1cm in diameter for swinger bars

*Dressed and in use.*

# 8

# TWO-TONE MEDIUM HORSE AND THE HOBBY HORSE

## TWO-TONE MEDIUM HORSE

As mentioned in Chapter 6, many people have difficulty finding suitable wood at a reasonable price, but most people can pick up plywood at DIY stores. Make sure it is good quality, although it is not necessary to use marine ply.

A medium-sized horse made from plywood is heavy, and the lime wood makes the joints at the top of the legs much stronger than they would have been with plywood alone. The Two-Tone Medium Horse follows the same construction method as for the Medium Standard Horse (*see* Chapter 4), but some of the plywood is laminated to beech for the legs or European lime for the body, giving an extra strong marbling effect to the finished horse. Check that the outside layer of plywood is the same dark colour all over to make the horse more attractive.

**Dimensions:** The same as the medium standard horse.
**Time taken:** 60 hours.

## MATERIALS

- Head: 3 × 435mm × 267mm × 25mm pieces of plywood
- Top: 1 × 660mm × 216mm × 25mm piece of plywood; 1 × 660mm × 216mm × 25mm thick piece of lime wood
- Bottom: 1 × 660mm × 216mm × 50mm piece of lime wood
- Sides: 2 × 660mm × 127mm × 25mm pieces of plywood; 2 × 660mm × 127mm × 25mm thick pieces of lime wood
- Ends: 2 × 116mm × 127mm × 25mm piece of plywood; 2 × 116mm × 127mm × 25mm piece of lime wood
- Front legs: 2 × 25mm pieces of plywood; 2 × 25mm pieces of beech wood
- Back legs: 2 × 25mm pieces of plywood; 2 × 25mm pieces of beech wood

Note: both sets of legs can be cut from one piece of plywood and one piece of beech wood, 255mm × 127mm × 25mm for each set.

- Hoof pads: 8 × 12mm pieces of plywood
- Inside front leg pads: 2 × 12mm pieces of lime wood
- Inside back pads: 2 × 12mm pieces of lime wood
- Outside front pads: 2 × 25mm pieces of plywood
- Outside back pads: 2 × 25mm pieces of plywood
- Rump pad: 1 × 25mm piece of plywood
- Cheek pad: 2 × 12mm pieces of plywood
- Neck pad (large): 2 × 25mm pieces of plywood
- Neck pad (small) 2 × 25mm pieces of plywood
- Hoof pads: 8 × 12mm pieces of plywood
- Studding: 2 × 230mm × 10mm diameter with 4 × washers and 4 × nuts (check length before cutting)

- 9mm doweling
- 2 × 25mm brown eyes
- 4 × M6 bolts – check length when horse is complete

## HEAD

(1) Cut out three head shapes (without the mouths) from the 25mm plywood.

Before the three layers of plywood are glued together, cut a 150mm long, 25mm wide slot from 25mm below the ears, right down the bridge of the nose, to make a flash down the horse's nose.

(2) Glue and clamp the three pieces of plywood together and cut out the mouth.

(3) Follow the instructions for the Medium Standard Horse (*see* Chapter 4)

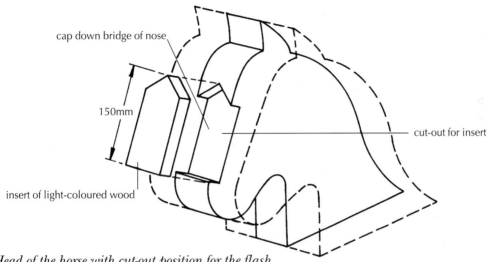

*Head of the horse with cut-out position for the flash.*

*Middle piece of head ply showing cut-out for flash.*

to put this horse together, bearing in mind that if the plywood is glued to a layer of lime wood, the lime wood is always on the inside of the body.

(4) Drill a hole for the eyes and a hole at the back of the mouth. Very carefully, saw the mouth for the teeth (a fine-toothed saw is best as there is less chance of the plywood crumbling).

*Tip*

If possible, clamp an odd piece of wood on the back of the head when drilling the holes to avoid the wood splintering when the drill comes through the other side.

(5) Glue on the cheek pads (one of the extra items that are on the plans).

(6) Sand the head into shape.

(7) When the face and ears are complete, glue and clamp on the first large neck overlays, and when those are dry add the two small overlays (see extra items on the

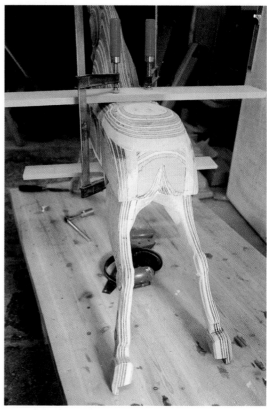

*How to clamp curved wood without marking the wood.*

plans). Plane the bottom flat and shape the neck, except for the very last few millimetres.

## BODY

(8) Put the head in place on the body and mark around the bottom. Also cut out the rump overlay and mark around its place on the body so that these areas are not sanded by mistake.

(9) Using the method described for the Medium Standard Horse, cut out the corners of the bottom plank in order to attach the legs (*see* chart on page 46).

(10) Glue on the head and the rump overlay. At 25mm, the rump overlay is too

*Head showing flash, ears and laminations.*

*Showing two-tone construction for the body of the horse.*

thick, so when it is dry sand off two layers of the plywood.

(11) Bolt the body together, and with a coarse cintride disc or similar, first coarse then finer sand the curves into the body, showing up the pale cream of the lime wood. By emphasizing the pale layers in the plywood, a design can be made on the chest and on the sides of the horse

## LEGS

(12) Glue and clamp the plywood and beech pieces together.

(13) Lay the leg patterns on the wood before cutting out the legs to make sure that they will be pairs; in other words, that the beech lamination is on the *inside* of all four legs and the darker wood of the plywood on the outside. Cut out all four legs and chamfer the tops, following the instructions given for the Medium Standard Horse, still checking that the beech wood is on the inside.

(14) Glue and clamp the eight hoof pads into place.

*The pattern of lamination showing up after sanding the breast.*

*Clamping inside leg overlays, plywood on outside of legs.*

(15) Sand the legs up to the line of the inside and outside overlays.

(16) Follow the instructions given for the Medium Standard Horse for the rest of the assembly.

# FINISH

Once the horse has been hand sanded, apply sealer and then varnish. The wood will feel very rough after the first seal and will need a second and a third seal with light sanding in between, followed by at least one varnish. Good hand sanding will get it smooth again before the last varnish.

*Tip*
Another horse can be made with the plywood on the inside and the lime wood on the outside, with the centre section of the

*Butting two pieces of mane together.*

head being the only piece of plywood in the head.

# SWINGER STAND

Use the sizes and instructions as for the Medium Standard Horse.

*Finished horse ready for tacking up showing the blaze down the nose and patter on the breast.*

*Finished horse showing the marked pattern on body and legs.*

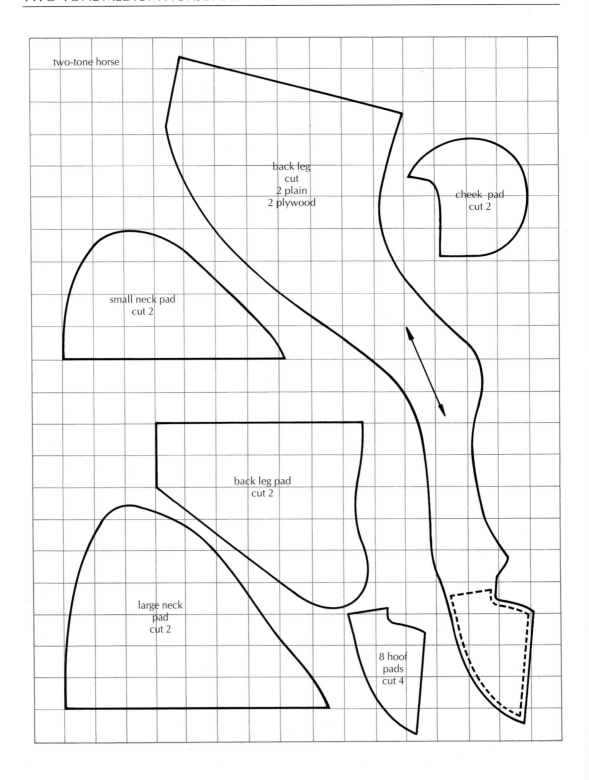

two-tone horse

back leg
cut
2 plain
2 plywood

cheek pad
cut 2

small neck pad
cut 2

back leg pad
cut 2

large neck
pad
cut 2

8 hoof
pads
cut 4

Each square is 25mm (1 inch) square

# HOBBY HORSE

This is not a rocking horse, but deserves a place among them as it was from the simple hobby horse that today's fine rocking horses have evolved. On the more practical side, the design is a way of using up off-cuts from larger projects.

# TOOLS

- Drill in a drill stand
- Hand drill and sanding discs
- 5mm, 16mm, 24mm drill bits (the last two can be spade drills)
- Paint brushes or air brush

# MATERIALS

- Head: 1 × 240mm × 85mm × 38mm good-quality piece of pine or plywood
- Pads: 2 × 95mm × 135mm × 25mm piece of softwood or plywood
- 1 × 150mm long × 14mm diameter doweling for the handles
- Pole made from a 50–70mm long broom handle, depending on the height of the child
- 2 × brown eyes, 14mm in diameter
- Fur fabric for mane and forelock
- 180mm × 6mm length of leather or leather cloth
- Decorative brass nails
- 2 × 50mm strong plastic wheels. Can be wooden-turned wheels but they need to be hardwood for strength

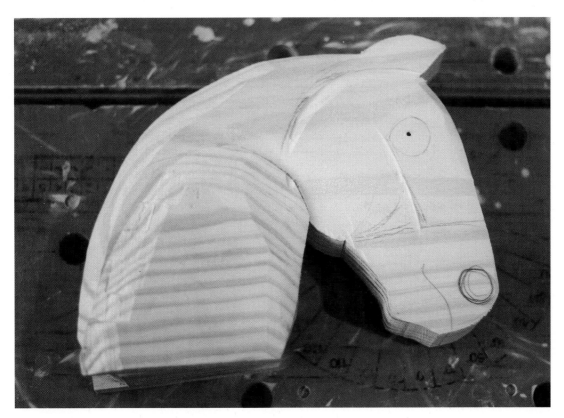

*Hobby horse head with pad glued on.*

- Metal spindle to fit wheels and hole through end of pole
- Washers and clips for the ends of the spindle

(1) Cut out the shape of the head and the two pads. Drill the pilot hole for the eyes through the head using the drill in the drill stand. Change the drill bit to the 16mm spade bit and drill a 5mm deep eye hole on each side of the head, taking the 5mm hole as a guide.

(2) Being careful to keep the head straight, drill a 24mm hole 40mm into the middle of the bottom of the head.

(3) Glue on the neck pads, as indicated on the plans.

(4) Drill the hole through the pads and head as indicated on the plans, except the doweling for the handles.

(5) Shape and sand the head and pads, and round the point of the ears. On each side of the nose, rub an area flat to indicate the nostrils.

(6) Fill the eye sockets with wood filler and press in the eyes, wiping away any excess to leave a round eye.

(7) Push the dowel about 50mm into the neck for the handles, coat the next 50mm with glue and then tap the doweling further through the horse until there is the same amount showing at each side. At the same time, coat the top 40mm of the broom handle/pole with glue and tap it into position. Leave both to dry.

(8) Leaving a strip on the forehead and one from the back of the ears and down the back of the neck free of all types of paint so that the forelock and mane will stick properly at a later stage, apply two

*Showing all the pieces needed for a hobby horse. The head is painted and the handles in place.*

*Wheels at the bottom of the pole.*

coats of sealer to the head, sanding between each one. Then apply primer, undercoat and a white enamel top coat. Leave the four coats of paint to dry while the hobby horse is held by its pole only.

(9) Paint the pole the colour of your choice using the same type of paint as for the head, and hang it up by the handles to dry. An overall coat of clear varnish will help to protect the horse from bumps and scrapes.

(10) Drill a hole 1–2mm larger than the spindle across the bottom of the pole in the same direction as the handles in the head, the height from the bottom being the height of the tyres on the wheels.

(11) Glue on the fur fabric forelock and mane.

(12) Nail the leather cloth strapping to the face with brass nails to form the bridle. An alternative is to use stronger leather and to extend the nose band to include short reins, omitting the handles in the neck.

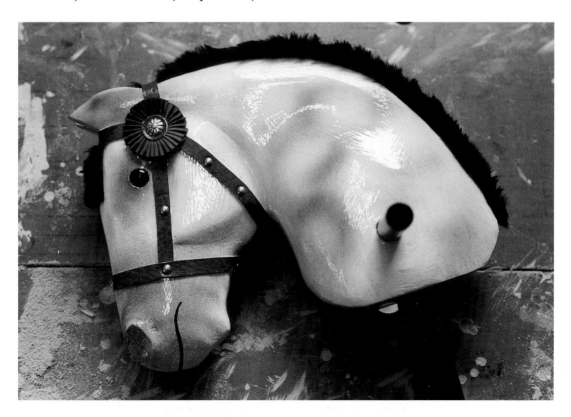

*Painted, tacked up and ready for its rider.*

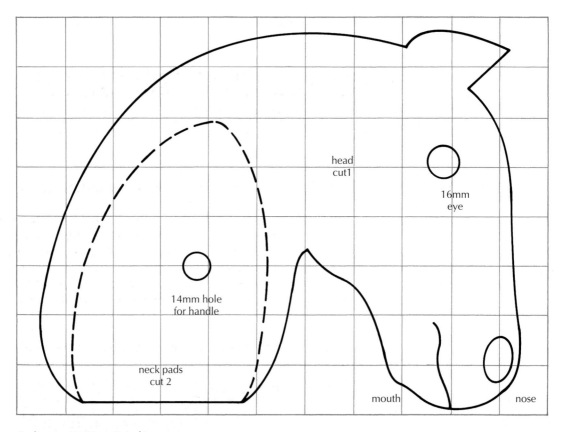

head
cut1

16mm
eye

14mm hole
for handle

neck pads
cut 2

mouth

nose

Each square is 25mm (1 inch) square

# 9

# EXTRA CARVED MEDIUM TROTTER

The Medium Standard Horse detailed in Chapter 4 is a strong horse, which should last for many years. If you would like something closer to reality, however, and have an itch to do some more carving, follow the instructions in this chapter in conjunction with those in Chapter 4 to create a horse that will be a fine piece of furniture as well as able to take the strain of endless hours of play. This horse is the same size as the Medium Standard Horse but has a thicker body and head to allow for the extra carving.

The woods seen in the illustrations are European lime for the head and body and beech for the legs and stand. Other woods can be used, but a good carving wood for the body and head and a strong, long grain hardwood for the legs, pillars and hoof rails or rockers are the most satisfactory. Colour-matching the woods if the horse is to be clear varnished or polished

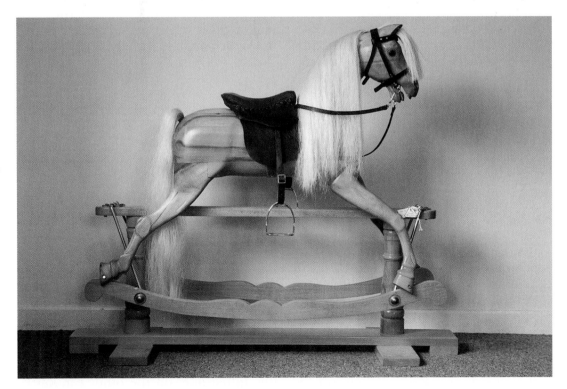

*Completed Extra Carved Medium Trotter on swinger stand.*

helps to co-ordinate it so that joints do not distract and everything flows from one muscle to the next, giving the look of a real horse. Using close up photographs of real horses can be a great help, although it must be remembered that, like us, every horse is slightly different.

# TOOLS

• As Chapter 4.

# MATERIALS

• Head: 1 × 320mm × 431mm × 104mm piece of softwood or hardwood
• Top plank: 1 × 660mm × 203mm × 51mm softwood or hardwood plank
• Side planks: 2 × 660mm × 128mm × 51mm softwood or hardwood planks
• End Plank (front): 1 × 128mm × 102mm × 77mm softwood or hardwood plank
• End plank (back): 1 × 128mm × 102mm × 102mm softwood or hardwood plank
• Bottom plank: 1 × 660mm × 203mm × 51mm softwood or hardwood plank
• Extra belly pad: 1 × 335mm × 165mm × 12mm piece of softwood or hardwood
• Rump pad: 1 × 191mm × 165mm × 12mm piece of softwood or hardwood
• Front outside leg (A): 200mm × 155mm × 12mm (if cut out separately following the contours of the leg) hardwood
• Front outside leg (B): 195mm × 150mm × 12mm (if cut out separately following the contours of the leg) hardwood
• Back outside leg (C): 161mm × 183mm × 12mm (if cut out separately following the contours of the leg) hardwood
• Back outside leg (D): 168mm × 155mm × 12mm (if cut out separately following the contours of the leg) hardwood
(For inside leg overlays use the plan for the outside overlays less 60mm off the

top of each one, to allow for the thickness of the bottom plank.)
• Hoof overlays: 8 × 165mm × 89mm × 12mm pieces of hardwood
• Leg (A) 2 × 546mm × 152mm × 20mm pieces of hardwood
• Leg (B): 1 × 622mm × 134mm × 38mm piece of hardwood
• Leg (C): 2 × 559mm × 172mm × 20mm pieces of hardwood
• Leg (D): 1 × 533mm × 134mm × 38mm piece of hardwood
• Neck overlays: 2 × 161mm × 205mm × 40mm thick pieces of softwood or hardwood (25mm longer for a turned head)
• 2 × brown glass eyes, 25mm in diameter

Note: legs (A) and (C) are each made from two pieces of 16mm thick wood; the grain of the wood of the two pieces should be offset on each leg (to make the leg strong). The other two legs (B) and (D) are 32mm thick and made from one length of wood with the grain running down the length of the legs.

### HEAD

The pattern at the end of this chapter has the head forward in a racing position, however you could use the pattern for the Medium Standard Horse if you prefer, but using the thicker wood.

(1) Cut out the pattern from a 100mm thick piece of wood. If using two 50mm thick pieces of wood, cut out one with the ear in a forward position and the other upright. Do not cut out the mouth until the two halves of the head are glued together.
(2) Mark in the lines as shown in Chapter 4. If using the 10cm thick piece of wood, saw out the centre between the ears to their base. On one ear, saw or chisel off to the dotted line; on the other ear, saw or chisel off the piece above the solid line.

This makes one ear appear to be forward, with the other slightly to one side. If using the 5cm-thick pieces of wood, it is easier to cut out the ears before the two halves are glued together. Saw off a slice across the front side of the ear, starting at nothing at the inner edge at the top and widening to 8mm at the bottom of the outer edge.

(3) Shape both ears at the back and sides as described in Chapter 4. Horses have a fold of skin from the inner bottom corner across the front of their ears almost to the outer edge, being three-quarters of the way across at the bottom and getting less until it disappears halfway up the front of the ear.

(4) Gouge out the rest of the front of the ear, about 4mm deep at the bottom corner and getting less and less nearer the tip, which is rounded for safety's sake.

There is a slight indentation from the tip, almost to the base, about 3mm from the back outer edge.

Note: the base of a real horse's ear is quite slender, but as the ears of a rocking horse are the most vulnerable points, the base is left quite thick for strength. Do not shape the area of the eyes until the eyes are carved.

## NOSE

(1) Take out a very narrow groove along the centre of the bridge of the nose, from just below the centre of the forehead to just where the nostrils begin to flair (if the head is made in two halves, the groove is at the end of the grain on both halves). Use a well-sharpened chisel or knife and

*Leave eye at this stage.*

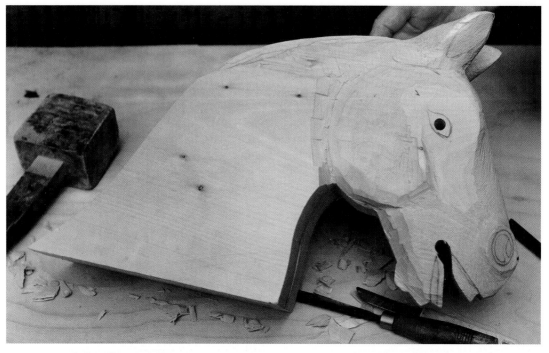

*Showing the turn of the ear, the shape the eye will be carved to and the line of the extra cut away for the tongue.*

take out no more than 1mm, leaving clean edges. Sand the groove which will round the edges. For further instructions, *see* Chapter 4.

(2) Curve the cheeks very slightly, from temple to jaw, rounding the jaw bone as it goes into the throat, where two almost parallel groves can be made to show where the gullet is before it disappears into the front of the neck.

## MOUTH

(1) When the cheek bone to jaw has been carved down to just over 62mm, continue this width along the sides of the mouth and round to the front, then mark in the teeth. Saw 4mm deep round each side of the lips as marked on the plans, to correspond with the front which is already cut away. Chisel off surplus wood and smooth with the flat of the chisel. On the actual lower teeth, saw another 4mm strip off all round, leaving the actual teeth as 5–7mm.

(2) Remove the surplus above this second cut, and carefully round the edges of the lump of wood left in the middle to make the tongue. This has no centre groove as it does in humans. Gouge out the palate leaving the same thickness of wood round the edge of the top teeth as the lower teeth; this creates the thickness of the upper teeth. There are only eight teeth in the upper jaw and eight teeth in the lower jaw that can be seen.

(3) Carefully sand, keeping the teeth and tongue clearly differentiated. Clean out the back of the mouth, and if the horse is to stay as plain wood, chisel a very narrow groove in between each tooth. A wide gap makes the horse look fierce, which is frightening to some children.

116

## EYES

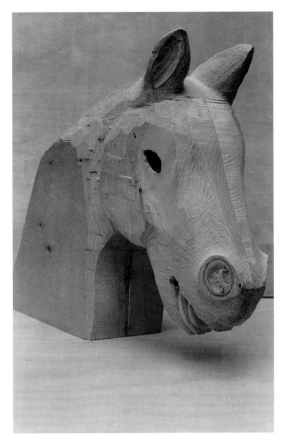

*Ear, eye, nose and tongue partly done.*

Before you start work on the eyes, practise carving an off-cut of wood until you are satisfied with the result. The eyelids are the last thing that are done on the head before the neck overlays are glued on.

(1) Mark in the eye socket using a pencil. The socket should be approximately 4cm long and 2cm at the widest point. It should be a slightly flattened lemon shape with the marker hole in the centre. One end of the lemon shape should point obliquely down the nose, the other towards the back of the head (so that if the horse had its head up, running at full gallop, the eye would be parallel with the ground to give perfect vision). Pencil in the eyelids – the top lid is about twice the width of the lower lid and both taper to nothing at the corners.

(2) Remove any wire from the back of the two eyeballs, making the backs as flat as possible. Using a freshly sharpened gouge, start gouging out the area of the eye socket, being careful not to go over the pencil lines of the lids.

*Dropping in the eye.*

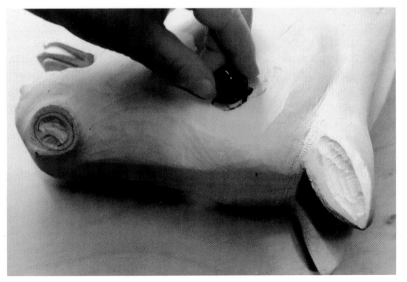

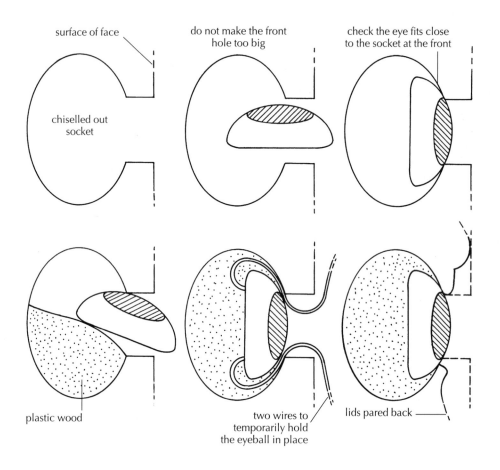

surface of face

chiselled out
socket

do not make the front
hole too big

check the eye fits close
to the socket at the front

plastic wood

two wires to
temporarily hold
the eyeball in place

lids pared back

*Inserting a glass eye into a carved eye socket.*

(3) Go half the width of the eye deep and then gouge out behind the upper and lower lids, carefully removing more wood from behind the top lid than from behind the bottom one, until the eyeball will slip under the top lid and very easily drop into place no more than 4mm below the edge of the bottom lid, so that the pupil is in the centre of the gap. The eyelids should still be about 3mm thick. At this point check that the eyeball is in good contact with the inside of both lids before proceeding; if not, gouge out more wood.

(4) Fill the lower part of the socket with plastic wood and, being careful not to get the plastic wood on the front of the eyeball, slip the eyeball into the top half of the cavity. Lift and press the eyeball so that it slots in behind the top and lower lid.

*Tip*
Do one or two dummy runs to practise putting the eyeball in place. An extra precaution is to use two hooked pieces of wire that are inserted in the corners and under the eye to keep the eye close to the lids until the plastic wood filler begins to

harden, as the eye is inclined to sink down into the plastic wood. Then carefully remove the wires and smooth over the plastic wood in the corners.

(5) The eyelids are best carved with something like a thin-bladed knife, as only thin slivers are taken off each time because it is so easy to take away too much and make a hole in the lid. The lid follows the actual curve of the eyeball into the corners, which are carved further into the wood; the corner of the eye nearer the nose is carved deeper as the rest of the wood becomes part of the side of the bridge of the nose. The top lid is more pronounced than the bottom one, with a deeper curve upwards, and the crease above is deep too, the upper side of the crease curving outwards to make the eyebrow. There are hairs on the eyebrow of a horse but they are not noticeable until one gets very close to, so they are disregarded. The lower lid is not so curved and the crease not so deep at the lower edge, having just a fold of skin before smoothing out as part of the cheek.

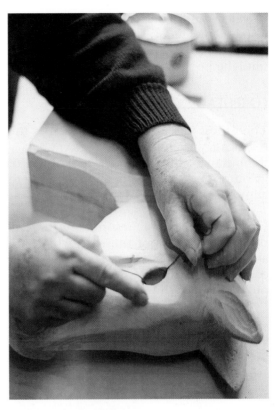

*Holding the eye up while the wood filler starts to dry.*

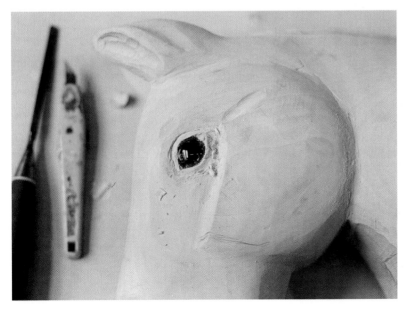

*Paring away the eyelids.*

119

(6) Fine sand, and fill any tiny gaps with wood filler. The eyes are now very vulnerable so tie a thick piece of cloth over them until the horse is complete.

## FOREHEAD

The widest part of the head is across the forehead, just above the eyes, and is a minimum of 90mm and a maximum of 100mm. The head has been made wide to allow for the carving of the eyes.

(1) The forehead slopes in from the eyebrows to the base of the ears, which are about 8mm across. There is a dent over each eye, and another dent from the temple (corner of the eye) runs towards the back of the ear, fading away after about 25mm. From the cheek bone, across the face, there are two more shallow grooves that finish by the nose and mouth.

## NECK

(For turned head only; use instructions in Chapter 4 for a straight head.)

(1) The overlays are now glued on. Note that they are different sizes depending which way you wish to have the head of the horse turned. On the side to which the head is to turn, glue the overlay flush with the front of the neck; on the other side, glue the overlay flush with the back of the neck.

*Showing the carved lines on the face.*

*Completed head ready to sand.*

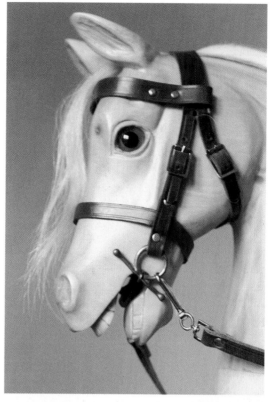

*Close up of eye and mouth when complete.*

(2) Turn the head upside down and draw a new centre line along the bottom which starts 90mm towards the overlay and finishes 90mm the other side of the old centre line at the back of the neck. Draw the 'egg' shape on the bottom (*see* diagram).

(3) At the front of the neck, ignore the old centre line and draw a new one from the bottom edge up on a curved slant as far as the throat, where it joins the original centre line. Likewise, there is a new curved centre line up the back of the neck to where it joins the old centre line, 100mm from the back of the ears.

(4) Chisel the spare wood away from the bottom edges of the neck first so there is a clear indication of the shape of the neck.

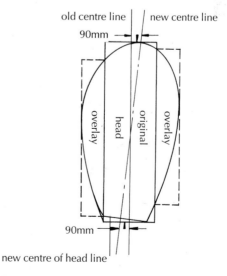

*Base of head show how to prepare to make it a turned head.*

*Mark in new centre line for a turned head.*

*Mouth details and marking on the bottom for a turned head.*

(5) The crest starts in the gap between the ears as just two small grooves, the width of the gap apart. Using the small gouge, make it deeper and wider as it goes over the top of the head following the new centre line. It should be 13mm deep and 20mm wide at its maximum, and then fades away to nothing by the time it gets to 60mm above the body, which is where the withers start.

(6) Behind the ears and above the cheek, the neck is 70mm thick, gradually sloping down and out to meet the already shaped bottom. Leave more of the overlay that is glued right to the back of the neck to show that the neck muscles are stretched more than on the opposite side. Sand away the lower edge of the crest so that it stands up from the head better.

(7) The withers start 60mm on the back of the neck above the body and slope in a ridge down the sides of the neck and into the muscles that slope down to the bunched muscles at the top of the front legs.

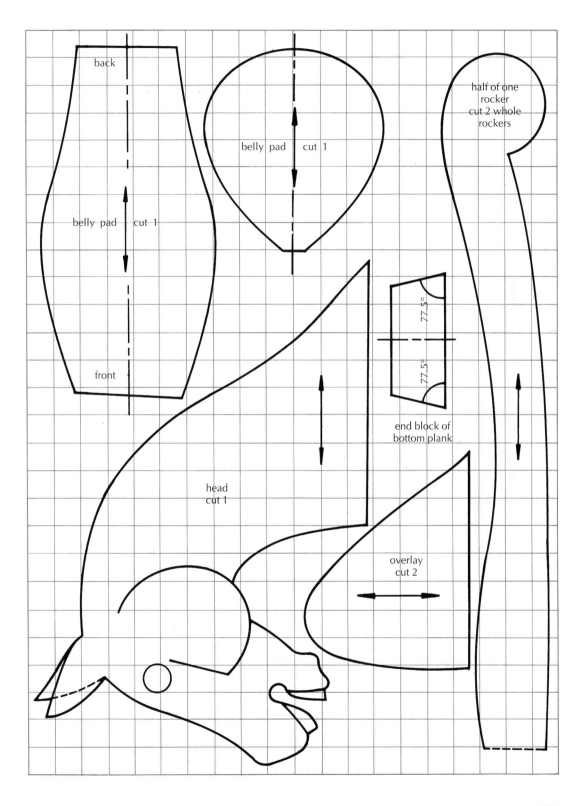

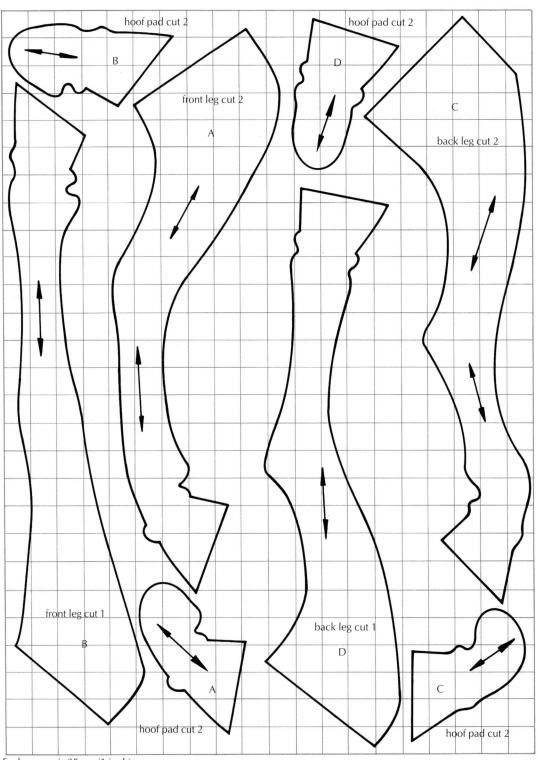

hoof pad cut 2

hoof pad cut 2

B

D

front leg cut 2

C

A

back leg cut 2

front leg cut 1

back leg cut 1

B

D

A

C

hoof pad cut 2

hoof pad cut 2

Each square is 25mm (1 inch) square

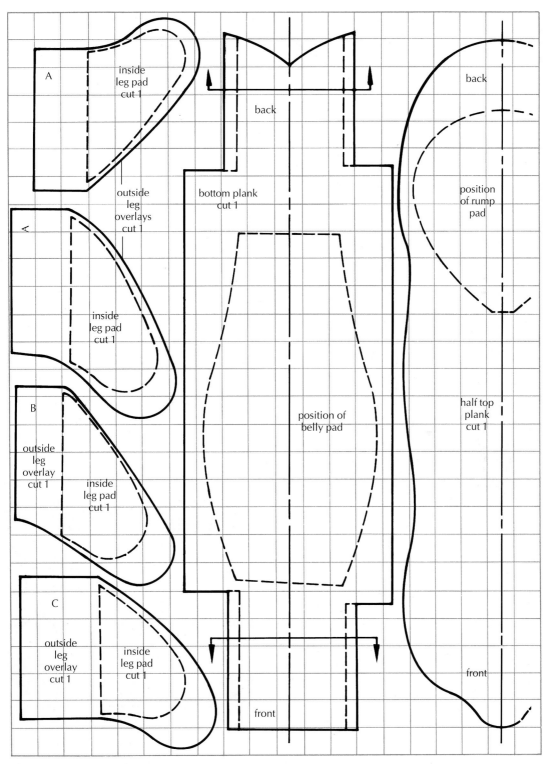

A

inside
leg pad
cut 1

back

back

position
of rump
pad

A

outside
leg
overlays
cut 1

bottom plank
cut 1

inside
leg pad
cut 1

B

position of
belly pad

half top
plank
cut 1

outside
leg
overlay
cut 1

inside
leg pad
cut 1

C

outside
leg
overlay
cut 1

inside
leg pad
cut 1

front

front

front

Each square is 25mm (1 inch) square

*Carving in 'strain' marks.*

## LEGS

(1) Glue together the two halves of both the bent legs; these look better at opposite corners of the body. Glue on the hoof pads. Mark round where the pastern meets the clench. Chisel and sand the clenches so that they are narrower at the top and slant wider where the shoe would be fitted.

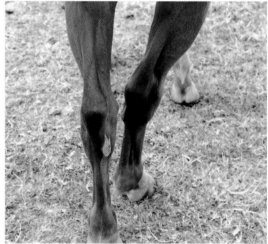

*A real horse's back legs.*

(8) Lightly sand the sides of the neck then carve grooves to represent the sinews in the neck, two on the side that the nose is turning away from, and one or two on the short side. Again, photographs of real horses can help you in placing these grooves in the right place. It is not the grooves that are important but the way the muscles 'round' into them.

(9) The head is now ready for final sanding, except for the bottom 60mm which is left until the head is glued onto the body.

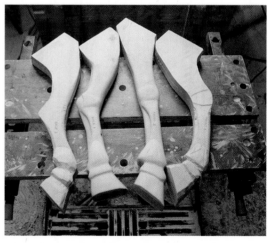

*Two stages of carving the legs.*

*Curve of the seat rump and back leg half done.*

(2) Round both clench and pastern as much as possible. Make the tendon groove up each side of the back of all four legs.

(3) Follow the illustration above to get the rounded point of the hock shape and the hamstrings going up the rest of the back legs. The front legs are similar to the design outlined in Chapter 4 but have a dent across the front of both knees which emphasizes their knobblyness.

## BODY

(1) Mark the bottom of the head on the top plank using the new centre lines. Also mark on the position of the rump overlay. On the bottom plank, mark the belly overlay, and also where the inside leg overlays will be.

(2) Bolt the body together. Carve the chest, ribs, and both rump and belly up to the markings for the overlays. Sand the areas just carved.

(3) Check whether the nuts are turning on the top ends of the bolts. If they are, peen over the ends of the bolts. Unbolt the body, glue on the head as in Chapter 4, but using the new centre lines also glue on the rump pad, not forgetting to insert the bolts first. Glue and bolt the body together, then finish and sand the rump.

(4) The saddle area can be left flat or carved away each side of a central spine ridge; the latter would need a saddle specially made for it.

(5) Screw and glue the legs on as for Chapter 4. When dry, clamp and glue on the outside leg overlays and belly pad. (If you can't clamp on the belly pad, use small screws round the edge where the holes can be sanded away.) Glue on all four overlays at the top of the legs as in Chapter 4.

(6) The front straight leg and the area above it has taut muscles and sinews. Starting at the withers the muscles go diagonally down the side of the horse, bunching at the front top of the leg above an inverted 'V' holding them in place. The path of two strong sinews show from just above the knee to the inverted 'V'.

(7) The bent leg shows similar muscles from the withers, across to only slightly bunched muscles above the leg. These are not so strained, however, the sinews not so deep, the 'V' at the top of the leg is much flatter, and there is only one sinew showing at the side between the knee and the inverted 'V'. The back bent leg has no strain showing on the side, and there is only a slight indentation between the top of the leg and the body. Also, looking from the rear, the rump is slightly lower

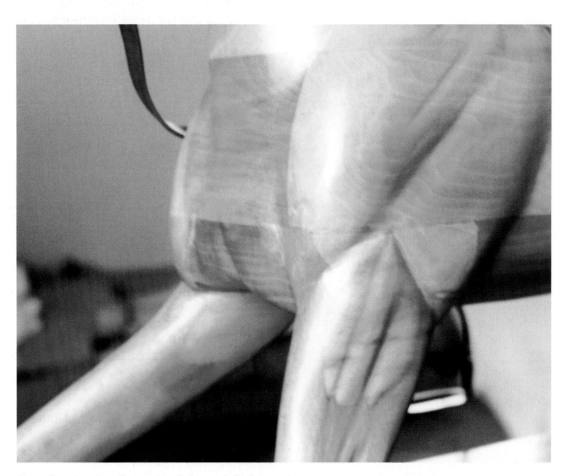

*Front leg showing the strain of the straight leg.*

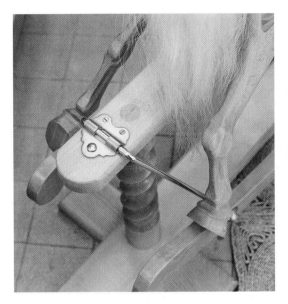

*Completed back legs with horse on stand.*

## BELLY

The belly overlay is mainly there to cover the ends of the bolts and give a little more depth to the rib cage.

(1) The lower ribs are carved round and behind the front legs, forward into the inverted heart shape on the chest, and up to the bottom of the neck.

(2) The belly near the back legs is carved deeper and rounds into the top of the leg, from which, in the opposite direction, there is the indentation that curves up the side of the horse to the point of croup.

These are indications of the extra carving that can be done on a horse. As discussed, studying real horses will no doubt provide some more subtle ways of embellishing a plain horse to give it extra interest and life.

Instructions for the rockers or stand are the same as those in Chapter 4, but the following illustrations give a few ideas as to how they can be custom-made.

on that side than on the side with the straight leg. On the stretched leg side there can be one or two shallow grooves at the top of the leg.

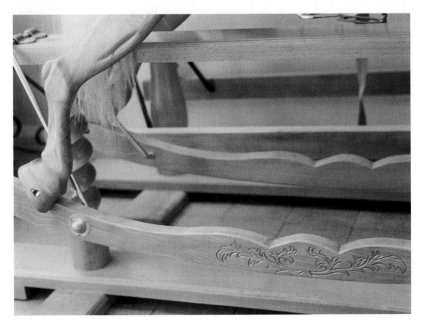

*One of many ideas to make pillars and hoof rails individual.*

*Ready to paint and tack up.*

*Tacked up and ready to go.*

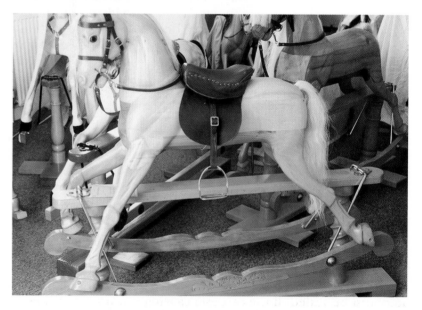

# 10

# LARGE ROCKING HORSE ON SWINGER STAND

This is a tall, majestic rocking horse, with its neck arched and strong muscles in the body and legs. It can also have details such as a tongue and palate, as described in Chapter 9.

Providing there is room – 3m of space is needed to allow it to swing freely – this horse is designed for all members of the family. It is large enough for a small, light-weight adult to ride, although a heavy teenage boy trying to win the Derby would do it no good at all. Yet it is gentle enough in movement for a young child (under supervision), and its back is quite long enough to allow two small riders to have lots of fun riding it together.

The gait of this horse is not suitable for use with rockers, therefore only details for a swinger stand are given.

**Dimensions:** 130cm high on its stand; 99cm to the top of the saddle; 74cm from breast to rump, grading it as large horse. It stands on a 175cm long swinger stand.
**Time taken:** a minimum of 60 hours to make, to which time for gluing and painting must be added. If the carousel carving is added, the time will increase further depending on how much carving is done.

## TOOLS

• As Chapter 4, except that the minimum length of the sash clamps is 3.1cm and the spade drill for the eye sockets is 32mm in diameter.

## MATERIALS

The head is tall so the main head (without overlays) can be made from two pieces of wood glued together along the grain of the wood before the head is cut out. Have the join at the top quarter of the head and securely doweled; it should never be at the bottom of the neck, which would also include the nose and make fine carving more difficult.

• Head: $1 \times 483mm \times 318mm \times 76mm$
• Top plank: $1 \times 735mm \times 230mm \times 50mm$
• Side planks: $2 \times 735mm \times 152mm \times 50mm$
• Bottom plank: (as top plank)
• End planks: $2 \times 127mm \times 152mm \times 76mm$
• Front legs: $2 \times 38mm$ thick
• Back legs: $2 \times 38mm$ thick
• $2 \times$ brown glass eyes, 28mm in diameter

An alternative for the head
If no 76mm wood is available, an alternative is to use two 50mm pieces of wood, equaling 100mm thick, in which case no cheek overlays are needed (this is much better if the horse is to have carousel carving). Narrow planks may be used for overlays, providing the two pieces for the large overlays are glued side by side before cutting out (not for carving).

two points suitable
to join two pieces
of wood together
to make a head

wrong place
to have a join

large horse

*Showing the right and wrong positions to join wood to make the head.*

Below are the sizes of wood needed if every overlay is to be cut from individual pieces of wood.

- Ears: 2 × 11.5mm × 3.8mm × 0.6mm
- Cheek/face: 2 × 15.2mm × 15.2mm × 0.9mm
- Large neck: 2 × 22.9mm × 25.5mm × 2.5mm
- Small neck: 2 × 12.1mm × 17.8mm × 2.5mm
- Shoulder: 2 × 25.5mm × 12.7mm × 1.3mm
- Ribs: 2 × 23mm × 12.7mm × 1.3mm
- Top rump: 1 × 20.3mm × 16.5mm × 1.9mm
- Side rump: 2 × 20.3mm × 12.1mm × 1.3mm
- Inside front leg: 2 × 8.9mm × 12.1mm × 1.9mm
- Inside back leg: 2 × 10.8mm × 13.3mm × 1.9mm
- Corner of leg: 4 × 6.4mm × 17.1mm × 3.2mm
- Outside leg front: 2 × 14mm × 17.1mm × 3.2mm
- Outside back leg: 2 × 16.5mm × 15.2mm × 3.2mm
- Hooves: 8,9 × 7.6mm × 1.3mm

Workshop space is needed when making this horse, as in the finishing stages there must be enough room to move the horse around in order to sand and paint it. It is heavy too, despite its hollow middle, especially when it is complete and on its stand, and is certainly not a rocking horse that you would want to constantly move around.

There is not a great deal of difference between actually constructing a large horse and a medium one, and you can therefore follow the instructions given in Chapters 4 and 5, with a few variations. Use the relevant numbered instructions below to replace the corresponding instructions in Chapter 4.

The most conspicuous difference between the two horses is that overlays are used for the large horse instead of making the wood thicker. This cuts down on cost, weight and construction time as a good proportion of the thicker wood would be carved away. The overlays have been made larger than necessary so that when the carving is being done there will be no 'edge' to interrupt when forming the muscles and curves. The edges and thickness of the overlays can be carved, sanded

*Work in progress using reclaimed timber.*

and smoothed away to nothing, or to whatever the maker requires. The depth of carving can also be greater because of these overlays, giving the strong, bold look that is typical of this design.

## HEAD

(1) Drill two 32mm diameter eye sockets 2mm deep (or 10mm deep if the head is 100mm thick with no cheek overlays). In other words, just deep enough to give a clear outline as to where the eyes will be fitted later.

(2) Cut and glue the overlays into position if 76mm wood is used for the head. The overlays allow room for a deep indentation (3mm) above the eye towards the forehead, and another shallow one by the temple reaching from the corner of the

eye up towards the back of the ear, fading to nothing close to the ear. The cheek can slope very gently, starting at the level of the eyes and sloping downwards until it ends with a very sharp dip at the lower end so that the wood is only 76mm thick across the back of the mouth. The large mouth allows room to manoeuvre the tools with which to carve a tongue, teeth and palate (*see* Chapter 9).

## EARS

Glue pads on the outside edge if 76mm thickness of wood is used for the head. The slot between the ears is 22mm. Looking from the front, the bottoms of the ears do not go straight across the head above the forehead but slope down. Each ear on the outside of the side of the head is

32mm and 25mm wide at the base. They go out to about 40mm wide, 35mm and are up from the bottom. For further details *see* Chapter 9.

## NECK

Glue each of the two overlays in turn, one large and one small, on each side of the neck (one large only each side if the thicker wood is used).

Starting between the ears, the crest of the head and neck is made by gouging out each side so that the back of the neck is only 19mm across and the channel runs down the neck each side of the crest for about 48cm, fading away to nothing at the lower end. From the inner edge of this channel, the sides of the neck slope gracefully outward and downward, leaving the last 35mm near the body to be carved when the head has been glued on to the body.

As the neck is arched, the tendons should show, including one running from the highest point of the cheek and sweeping in a curve down the side of the neck. Follow the instructions given in Chapter 9 for carving the neck, and for any other extra carving of the head.

## BODY

The middle section of the body should measure approximately 74cm × 23cm × 15cm when glued together, plus the overlays which are glued in the positions marked on the plans. The four overlays, that are glued into the corners next to where the tops of the outside overlays of the legs will be, are best glued on when the latter are in place. These will be on the sides of the bottom plank and help to give shape to the line between body and leg.

Before carving the underside of the body, fit, carve and sand the inside overlays on the legs so that the carving and sanding can be done right up to them.

*Large horse finished and ready to go.*

## LEGS

Follow the instructions in Chapter 4, using the open socket method.

## ASSEMBLY

Follow the instructions given in Chapter 4, adding the following to instruction (8):

Towards the top of the front outside legs, two sinew grooves go from about 50mm above the knee up to the bunched muscles above the leg. These show up quite clearly and are different from the back legs which have one sinew groove 10mm from the inner edge of the leg and about 100mm long. The rest of the leg consists

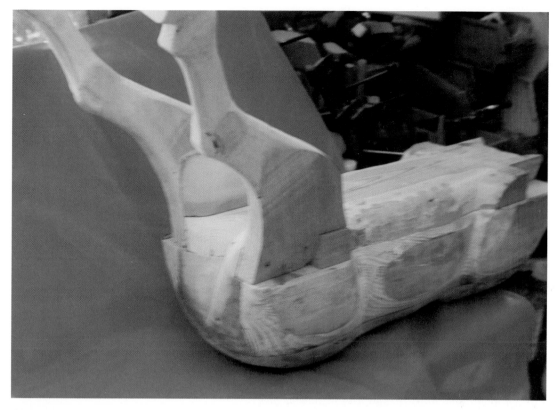

*Showing the extra overlays down the side and the extra piece of wood at the top of the back leg.*

of thick muscle right across, except for the hamstring at the back, and shows only a slight dip between the leg and body muscles. *See* Chapter 9 for details of carving muscle details.

## SWINGER STAND

All sizes and guidelines can be found in the charts and diagrams in Chapter 5. The pillars and hoof rails must be of hardwood, the swinger bars are 12mm in diameter and the two clamps must be able to take the 13mm swinger bars.

## ACCESSORIES

Possible accessories include mane and tail, bridle, bit, reins, saddle, stirrup straps, stirrups, saddle cloth, martingale and cropper strap. The options are very much open for this size of horse, so refer to the Accessories section in Chapter 4 before deciding on type and colour. For example, if you are making a horse that will be used for older children as well as younger ones, it is ideal to have a custom-made removable saddle, as well as a removable bridle and martingale; if it is for a school or somewhere similar, it is more practical if everything is nailed on so that items will not get lost. This decision should be made before carving com-

*Large dappled grey, brass fittings and removable tack.*

mences, because if everything is going to be removable the body may have to be drilled or carved to fit the saddle, depending on the type of removable saddle used.

# CAROUSEL CARVING OF A HORSE

Another alternative for anybody who would like to do more carving is to decorate your horse in a similar fashion to a carousel horse. This can make even a medium-sized horse look very dramatic.

The horse should be made of a good carving wood. Traditionally, the carousels were made of European lime, which is 15–25mm thick, with no overlays on the body.

Note: the sockets for the legs will have to be the same distance apart across the horse or the hooves will not fit on the hoof rails; the overlays will be that much deeper on the outsides of the legs to correspond.

The carving on a good carousel horse was not just painted on, it was actually carved into the wood. It has a flamboyant, larger than life appearance, and is very often done to a theme, such as garlands of flowers, birds, animals, nursery rhymes (for example 'Oranges and Lemons...'), ribbons, the flowing cloth of the medieval days, geometric designs and some that are not so geometric. Anything that is eye catching and interesting is ideal. A book on carving can help with ideas and details.

*The neck of a carousel. The little cherub is holding the wide ribbon for the name.*

There are a few things to be wary of, the most important being that in your enthusiasm for carving you do not leave any edges or points that can harm. The mane can be flowing free but it can still be safely controlled. Assuming that children will use the horse, the chest and rump can be used for the deeper carving, while flatter items such as cloth, saddle flaps and straps can be carved on the horse's flanks, made so as not to rub little legs. If it is just going to be a show piece, there is no limit.

Traditionally, the horse was white or occasionally black, and the carved mane was either yellow or gold; a long tail was cream or black horse hair. The backrest that sloped up from the back of the carved saddle ended in a scroll, or something so carved that there was a good handhold for the showman who had to move the (heavy) horses from place to place. The legs were always tucked up as they never touched the ground; all movement was through the brass pole, but the patterns in

*The seat backrest has been carved into a cherub that is also a hand hold.*

*Themes on carousel horses: at the back 'Treasure Island', at the front the rhyme 'Oranges and Lemons'. Note that the seats are left free of carving.*

this book of course show the legs spread out for rocking.

As some of the carving will need more wood in addition to the extra thickness that is on the body, for example a dragon's tail curled round a back leg, the extra 'lump' can be cut out as an extension of the leg, however sometimes pieces have to be glued on. It is important to plan the carving before any wood is cut, and then to mark it out on the actual place it will be carved so that balance and size can be co-ordinated. Doing some carving on an odd piece of wood will give an idea of the depth of carving you are going to do.

Very little carving was done on the side of a carousel horse that the fairground goers never saw, but for a carousel horse that is also a rocking horse, feel free – it doesn't simply have to be a repeat of the other side.

## HEAD

(1) Cut out the head with an extra wavy edge and an extra 25mm of crest to allow for carving the mane. Also leave an extra 12mm thickness of wood going down the length of the forehead only, with which to carve the forelock.

(2) After marking in the eyes, round the throat and front of the neck, next glue on the neck overlays (you will also need the leg overlays but not on the body). Then start carving your design, with the horse

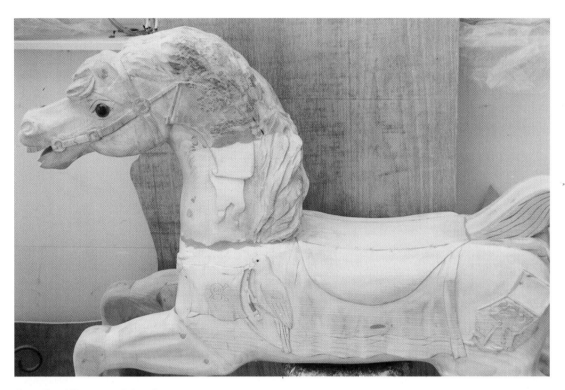

*Details of Treasure Island.*

*A figurehead for a backrest.*

still in its sections of head, body and legs to make for ease of mobility. Keep in your mind's eye the horse that is under the decoration so that you keep the sense of proportion. Do not go too deep when carving, and there should be a definite inner edge to all the decoration so that when painting there is a clear line to follow.

(3) As there are no reins on a carousel horse (a removable bridle can be put on for riding), rings were carved in the corner of the mouth and a strap carved with a big buckle going up to the temple and then over the top of the head and hair to the temple and mouth on the other side. A decoration was carved at the temple on the left-hand side, and a streamer came down the neck with the horse's name painted on it.

## BODY

(1) Around the back of the rump, traditionally there was always a swag of cloth, flowers or something in a loop under the tail. Underneath the scrolled backrest is another place for deep carving; the sides of the rump can also take deep carving.
(2) On the flanks the carving should simulate the leather saddle and flaps, and the saddle cloth and trimmings. The ideas are endless, depending on your carving expertise. Deep, flamboyant carving can be done on the breast and rump, away from the position of a child's knee.
(3) When the design and carving are well under way, then is the time to add the lines of the rocking horse itself, as described in Chapter 4.

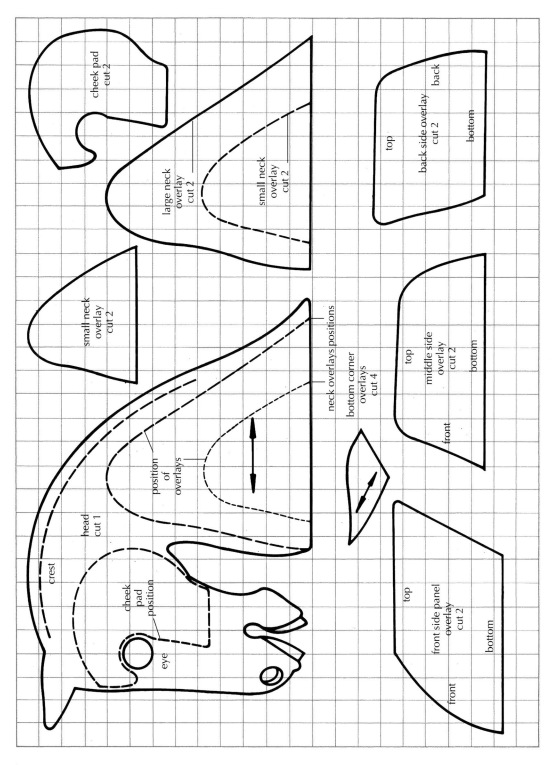

Each square is 25mm (1 inch) square

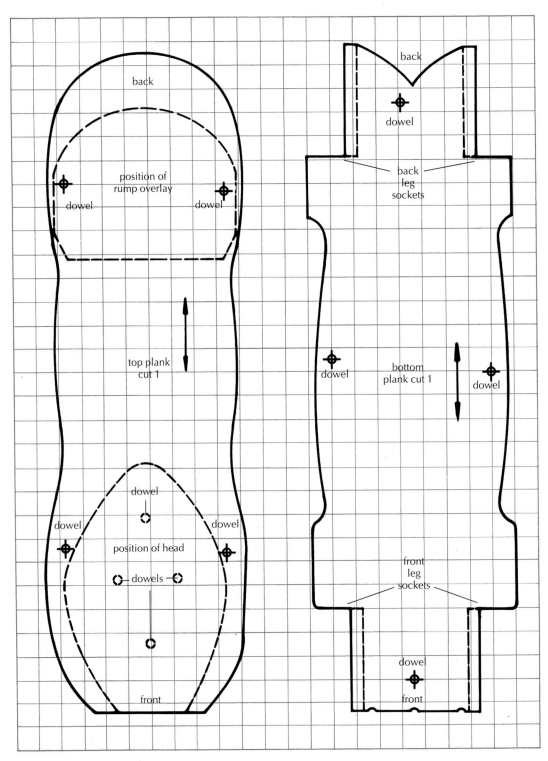

Each square is 25mm (1 inch) square

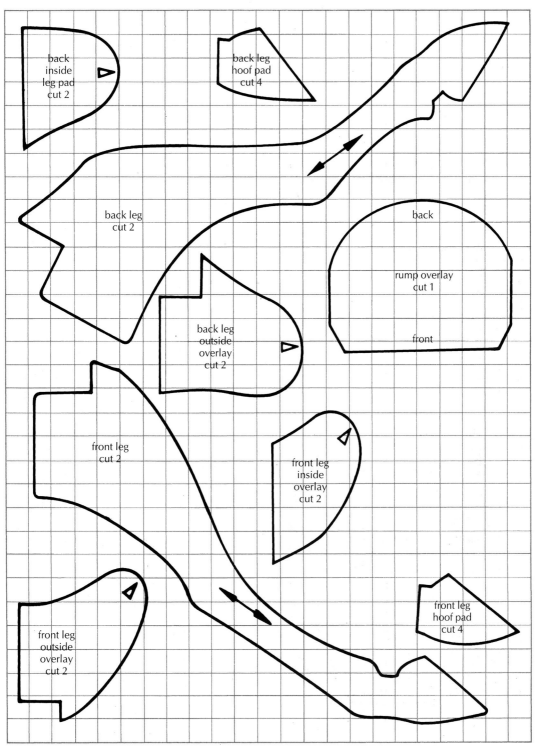

back
inside
leg pad
cut 2

back leg
hoof pad
cut 4

back leg
cut 2

back

rump overlay
cut 1

front

back leg
outside
overlay
cut 2

front leg
cut 2

front leg
inside
overlay
cut 2

front leg
outside
overlay
cut 2

front leg
hoof pad
cut 4

Each square is 25mm (1 inch) square

143

# TINY CARVED HORSE

Imagine a horse stretched out in full gallop but carved in miniature. What a beautiful ornament for any home, or to complement a collection of dolls. This horse is a delight for a woodcarver.

Designed for carving with the difference that it follows the style of the traditional rocking horse by having a real hair mane and tail, it is also painted, although it could be left as plain wood and varnished or polished.

Any type of wood suitable for carving can be used; in this case it is European lime, one of the easiest woods to carve. The carving can be done to any degree

that the carver wishes. The horses illustrated are only carved to a moderate degree to show how a minimal amount of carving can be very effective. Extra fine details can be included, such as carving the shoes on the back hooves, but very fine carving tools will be required for this type of work.

As with the large rocking horse, the legs are splayed for stability and made separately from the body so the grain of the wood is straight down the delicate legs.

The horse cannot be used as a normal toy as the legs are likely to break if it is dropped. It is tempting to display the horse in a window, which is fine if the hot sunshine is not streaming through. The horse should be kept away from any concentrated source of heat, such as a radiator.

**Dimensions:** Overall length with rockers 762mm; overall height 365mm.
**Time taken:** 15–20 hours, depending on how much detailed carving is done.

## TOOLS

(For a horse with only moderate carving.)

- Bandsaw or equivalent
- Tenon saw
- Plane or planer
- Twist drills – 3mm, 4mm, 9mm and 12mm
- Electric hand drill
- Medium screwdriver
- 6mm and 12mm × No. 8 gouges
- 6mm and 9mm flat chisels

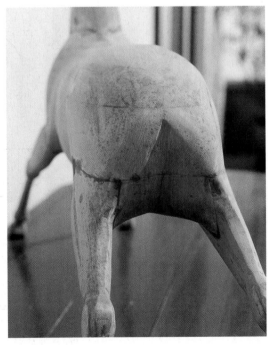

*Carving of the rump.*

- Rifler files
- Round surform
- Sanding paper, from coarse to extra-fine

Other tools, such as a power file and a selection of miniature wood carving tools would also be helpful.

# MATERIALS

All the wood is European lime, except for the rockers and spacer bars. Very soft pony or cow hair still on the hide is used to make the mane and tail.

- Top plank: 1 × 305mm × 100mm × 70mm or 2 × 305mm × 100mm × 45mm
- Bottom Plank: 1 × 305mm × 100mm × 50mm
- Front leg: 1 × 230mm × 76mm × 50mm (to be split in two later)
- Back leg: 1 × 203mm × 76mm × 50mm (to be split in two later)
- Head: 1 × 210mm × 140mm × 45mm
- Neck overlay: 2 × 89mm × 50mm × 9mm
- Rockers: 1 × 762mm × 127mm × 38mm piece of hardwood (to be split in two later)
- Spacer bars: 3 × (approximately) 89mm long × 12mm diameter pieces of hardwood
- Screws
- Glue
- 12 × pin nails to fix the mane
- Sealer, varnish, paint or polish

Note: the top plank can be made of two thinner planks if necessary. The bottom should be kept at the thickness of the top of the legs, either plynth or racer. Two planks only are recommended for a horse that is to be left plain wood and not painted at all. The legs can be cut from one piece of wood (254mm × 102mm × 50mm) because of the need to match the leg tops and leg sockets accurately.

## CONSTRUCTION FOR RACER

Before any construction is done, read through Chapter 4, as this horse is made in much the same way as the Medium Standard Horse, and the same principles apply.

(1) Plane the wood to be used for the head and cut out the silhouette. Drill a 9mm hole through the head to form the back corner of the mouth, as indicated on the plans. Cut out the mouth.

(2) Cut out the two (or three) planks for the body, and plane the top and bottom of each. Cut out one rocker and only one front and one back leg shape from the 50mm wood. Plane each leg down the sides, then mark down the centre of its length and cut along this line to divide each one into a pair of legs (only slightly wider than needed). In this way each pair of legs is exactly the same, making it easier

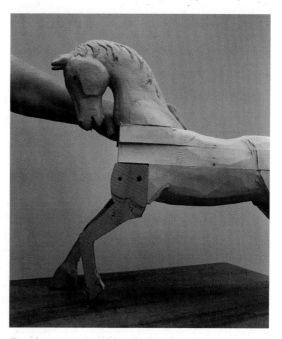

*Partly constructed horse showing the alternative of a carved mane.*

*Partly constructed horse showing a carved tail.*

to get the horse to stand evenly. Do not finish the carving of the feet until this is the case, and no more needs to be taken off the bottom of the hooves.

(3) Screw the body together with holding screws. For the plain wood version, screw from the underneath only. Draw a line along the centre of the back, down the breast, along the belly and up the rump.

(4) Draw a similar line up the back of the neck and head, over the ears, down the centre of the bridge of the nose, over the mouth and chin, down the centre of the throat and the front of the neck.

(5) Unscrew the body and cut out the sections in the corners of the bottom plank to make the leg sockets.

(6) Screw the body back together. Mark the contours of one side of the horse, as shown on the plans, and cut away the surplus wood.

(7) From the underside of the top plank, screw the head on with two screws. Screw the rest of the body and legs together using the planed side of each leg as the inside.

(8) Stand the horse up to make sure that it is standing evenly on its legs. If the horse is to stay in plain wood, the legs can be clamped on temporarily so that no screw

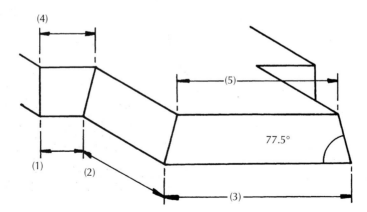

*Bottom plank of the tiny, medium and large horse (see chart on page 46).*

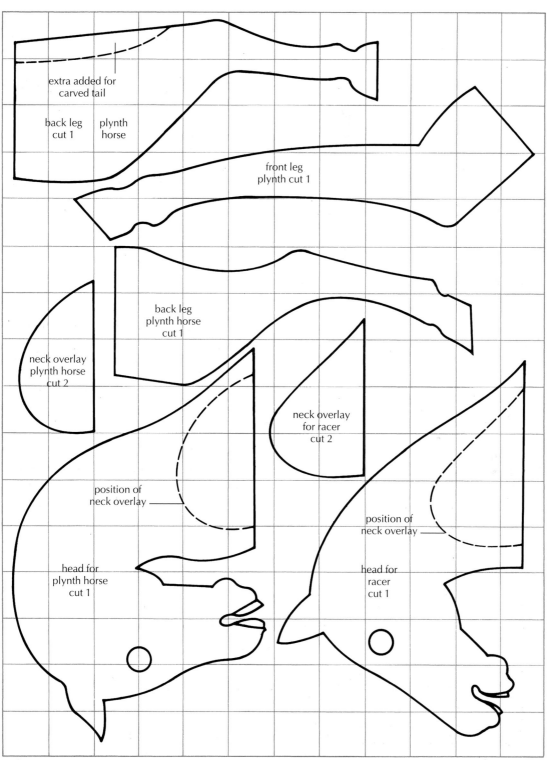

extra added for
carved tail

back leg
cut 1

plynth
horse

front leg
plynth cut 1

back leg
plynth horse
cut 1

neck overlay
plynth horse
cut 2

neck overlay
for racer
cut 2

position of
neck overlay

position of
neck overlay

head for
plynth horse
cut 1

head for
racer
cut 1

Each square is 25mm (1 inch) square

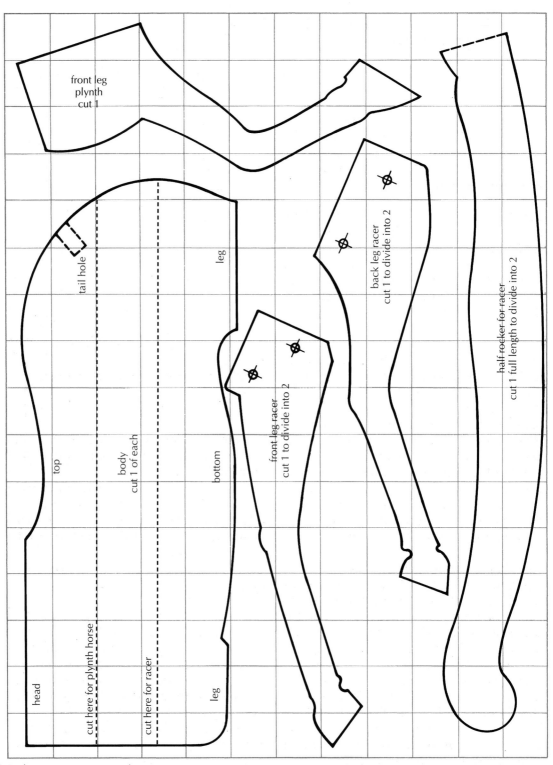

front leg
plynth
cut 1

tail hole

leg

top

body
cut 1 of each

bottom

leg

head

cut here for plynth horse

cut here for racer

front leg racer
cut 1 to divide into 2

back leg racer
cut 1 to divide into 2

half rocker for racer
cut 1 full length to divide into 2

Each square is 25mm (1 inch) square

holes will show in the tops of the legs. Adjust the legs if necessary.

## CARVING

The main carving can now begin. Measurements given in the carving instructions are only the outside limits for the carving; as horses come in many shapes and sizes, you may prefer to slim down your horse a little.

(1) The legs are carved separately from the body. The hooves should be no more than 19mm across, while the width of the leg just below the knee or hock is 16mm. The top of the legs are chamfered slightly to fit well into the leg sockets in the bottom plank.

*Tip*
When shaping the legs, leave the hooves and pastern unshaped until the legs have been attached to the body and checked. As there is so little wood, a mistake may mean making a whole new leg, so check that all four legs fit properly on the rockers before doing the final carving.
(2) Drill a 4mm pilot hole horizontally through the head where the centre of the eye is marked on the plans. This ensures that the eye will be in exactly the same position on both sides of the face.

(3) When carving the head, extra-fine detail can be added depending on the wood used. These can include such features as a tongue and palate, and the underside of the cheek bone and throat. To keep the head in proportion, the forehead just above the eyes should not be more than 44mm across, and the back of the mouth 28mm across. The nostrils should flare as the horse is in the full gallop position, so from one outside edge of the extended nostril across the nose to the other extended nostril should be no more

*Checking how much to carve off the front hoof.*

than 32mm. Across the widest part of the front of each ear is 11mm, tapering to 8mm at the base.
(4) For the body, follow the instructions in Chapter 4, not forgetting that the underside of this horse can be seen just as easily as any other part and should therefore be finished with the same care.

## SANDING

There is only a small amount of sanding that can be done with an electrically operated sander, as they are too fierce for such a small object, so unless you have specialist equipment for fine carving, do it by hand using surform and rifler files. Also, sand by hand using coarse paper and gradually using finer and finer paper. Leave the very last sanding for when the entire horse has been glued together.

*Marking up the pieces.*

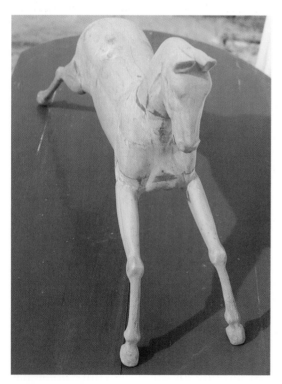

*Final sanding.*

## ASSEMBLY

(1) From underneath, glue and screw the head to the top plank, and when dry remove the screws and replace with dowels. Glue and screw the body and legs together, or if the horse is to be plain wood, glue and clamp the legs in place, putting pads behind each clamp to stop the wood getting bruised. When dry, replace the screws with dowels. Take care not to put any sideways pressure on the legs. Finish by doing any final shaping to smooth over the joints, check if any wood filler is needed and then give it the final sanding.

## FINISH

Follow the suggestions in Chapter 4 for painting the horse.

## ROCKERS

(1) Sand the whole of the rocker. Drill three holes 4mm in diameter horizontally through the sides of the rocker, as indicated on the plans, and countersink both sides.

(2) Draw a line down the centre of the length of the rocker and saw down this line to make two 19mm wide rockers. Plane the sawn-off side of the rockers. If you are making decorative rockers, the effect is better if the spacer bars are of the same wood as the horse and can have turned detail. If this is not possible, 12mm doweling can be used instead.

(3) Rest the horse on the rockers, slightly forward of the middle so that the horse will not tip to the front, propping up the rockers if necessary. The hooves must be right on the rockers and not overlapping the sides. The measurements of the three spacer bars are the measurements between the rockers. Cut all three to the exact

length and, making pilot holes first, glue and screw them into position with 25mm × No. 6 countersink screws. Check that the rockers are squared up. Cover the heads with wood filler.

(4) When dry, place the horse back on the rockers in the correct position. It will be seen that a portion of the underside of each hoof needs paring away so that it makes good contact with the rocker and still leaves the horse steady. The idea is to put a 12mm × No. 4 screw from the top of the hoof through into the rocker to firmly anchor each leg, so great care must be taken over the whole operation to avoid damaging the legs.

(5) When the hooves are sitting flat on the rockers to your satisfaction, put a small pilot hole through the top of each hoof and into the rocker, as near vertical as possible. The back hooves may have to be drilled through the back of the hoof instead of the top. Take the horse off the rockers and make the hole in each of the

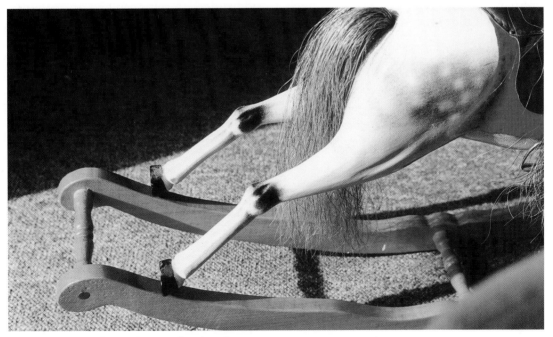

*Back legs screwed to rockers and painted over.*

hooves just big enough to take a No. 4 screw. Then countersink the top, which is better done by hand as there is so little thickness that the countersink bit is likely to go straight through the hoof. Return to the rockers and fix with screws, then cover the top with wood filler.

## MANE AND TAIL

(1) The mane is cut from the softest hair of a young pony or cow tail, with the hair still attached to the hide. If the hide is too thick, skive some of it away with a very sharp, thin-bladed knife to make it thinner and more pliable. Soak the tail and then cut one strip 160mm × 7mm, and another 20mm × 7mm, cutting through the hide side. Nail the short piece behind the ears, with the hair falling between the ears and down the bridge of the nose. The long piece is butted to the short piece behind the ears (this is an ideal spot at which to have the bridle strap cross the top of the head) and is nailed down the crest so that the hair falls over the neck, stopping at the withers.

*Tip*
If the hair sticks up, put a damp cloth over it for a few days.

(2) Drill a 12mm diameter and 19mm deep tail hole in the centre of the rump, in line with the back of the neck, as indicated on the plans. Cut long hair from the rest of the tail, apply glue to the cut end, and while it is gathered in a bunch wind a long length of cotton thread round the hair and glue. If it is not big enough to fill the tail hole, add some more hair until it is a good fit, then add some more glue and smear glue into the tail hole as well. Push the tail in as far as possible, wipe away any glue that has oozed out, and leave to dry.

## ACCESSORIES

The rocking horse will look beautiful with no adornment other than its mane and tail, but accessories such as stirrups, perhaps a saddle cloth to give colour, a saddle and bridle with reins can give an authentic finishing touch.

*Ready for the Derby.*

Fine leather that is only 1mm thick is best for making all the leather accessories. The stirrups should have a 25mm wide sole. The saddle cloth can be made of fine felt with a thin braid round the border. Using 6mm long, small-headed brass nails to fasten the saddle and bridle is in keeping with the dome nails used for the large rocking horse.

# A HORSE ON A PLINTH OR A UNICORN

Included in the plans is an alternative design – a horse with an arched neck, one bent front leg, one back leg with an extra piece at the top used to carve part of a tail, and one front and one back leg in normal standing positions, is different from the rocking horse. Add an extra 10mm to the back of the body if the tail is to be carved.

(1) Dispense with the rockers for this horse and mount it on a plinth instead.

*A unicorn for display only.*

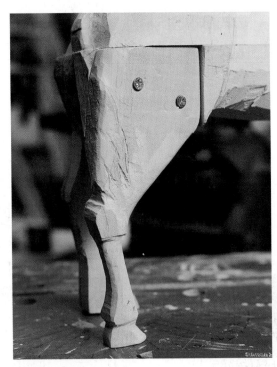

*Starting to carve the tail.*

*Assemble.*

*Marking the twist of the horn of the unicorn with thread.*

Cut the sockets for the legs in the bottom plank; these should be straight with no angle so that the legs are not spread but straight down from the body.

(2) The horse is made in the same way as the Tiny Carved Horse, except that the head is at a different angle and the horse is only screwed to the plinth by three legs. A free-standing horse is possible but not very steady. If you intend to carve a mane and tail, add an extra thickness to one back leg and 10mm on the rump for the tail.

(3) The horse is now ready for the final shaping. The mane should be carved before the neck, but after the face has been carved as normal.

(4) A further embellishment is to make the horse with its arched neck into a unicorn. Shape a piece of lime into a cone with the grain of the wood along its length. This should be 45mm long and 6mm in diameter at the base, with a 4mm stub on the end to fit into a small hole drilled into the forehead. Leave this step until just before the horse is painted so that the horn does not get in the way or get damaged. (The sizes given are approximate as everyone's idea of the size of the horn seems to be different.)

(5) Sand the cone. Attach a piece of cotton or fine string to the butt with blue-tac

*Tiny carved horse on rockers.*

(or similar) and wind it up the cone in a spiral.

(6) Mark up the cone along the cotton spiral. Cut out the groove of the spiral quite deeply. Sand, then put glue on the stub end and push it into the hole in the forehead, and leave to dry. It might take a few attempts to get the angle of the horn and spiral to your liking.

The plinth is an oblong piece of wood that is heavy enough to make the horse stable.

# FURTHER INFORMATION

## BOOKS

Dew, Anthony, *Making Rocking Horses*, ISBN 0 7153 861 4

Dew, Anthony, *The Rocking Horse Maker*, ISBN 0 71530 086 5

Dinger, Charlotte, *The Art of the Carousel*, ISBN 0 91450 7 00 1

Fawdry, Marguerite, *Rocking Horse Manufacture*, ISBN 1 87272 706 9

Green, Clive and Dew, Anthony, *Restoring Rocking Horses*, ISBN 0 94681 928 7 (HB), 0 94681 931 9 (PB)

Mullis, Patricia, *The Rocking Horse*, ISBN 0 90456 869 5

Spencer, Margaret, *Rocking Horses*, ISBN 1 85223 454 7 (HB), 1 86126 182 9 (PB)

Some of these books may be out of print now, but it is worth looking in your local library or finding a second-hand one.

## USEFUL ADDRESSES

### THE BRITISH TOY MAKERS GUILD

124 Walcot Street, Bath, BA1 5BG

The British Toy Makers Guild will give information about toy safety, such as suitable paints and other materials. To become a member your work has to pass a panel, who judge it for craftsmanship, originality, and safety.

Many counties have their own craft guilds who welcome new members, but again your work has to pass a panel of members who judge your work on craftsmanship, originality and safety. This keeps the quality of work produced at a high standard. They also organize their own exhibitions.

## THE GUILD OF ROCKING HORSE MAKERS

The Rocking Horse Shop, Fangfoss, York, YO41 5JH

The Guild of Rocking Horse Makers has a more relaxed approach, welcoming anyone who has made a rocking horse to become a member. They can also give details of the quarterly Rocking Horse and Toy magazine

## MARGARET SPENCER AND CO.

Chapel Cottage, Howe Green Road, Purleigh, Essex CM3 6PZ

A large range of accessories specifically made for rocking horses; mail order welcome.

## K.TOYS

Westfield Trading Estate, Midsomer Norton, Bath, BA3 4BH

Child-safe paint

# OTHER SOURCES OF INFORMATION

Bethnel Green Museum of Childhood, London have a good display of old rocking horses.

Pollocks Toy Museum, London also has rocking horses. The Museum of Childhood in Edinburgh has quite an early horse, and other museums around the country usually have one or two old rocking horses if they include a nursery or childhood section in their displays. Many large toyshops have rocking horses on display, especially at Christmas time. Large craft fairs very often have a stall of rocking horses, and some even have the craftsman working on the stall who is usually only too willing to answer questions - even if it is only to give them a five-minute break!

# INDEX